THE
UNDERSTANDING
YOUR SUICIDE GRIEF

Support
Group

GUIDE

[SECOND EDITION]

T0274636

Companion
P R E S S

Companion Press is dedicated to the education and support
of both the bereaved and bereavement caregivers. We believe that those
who companion the bereaved by walking with them as they journey in
grief have a wondrous opportunity: to help others embrace and
grow through grief—and to lead fuller, more deeply-lived lives
themselves because of this important ministry.

For a complete catalog and ordering information, write or call:

Companion Press
The Center for Loss and Life Transition
3735 Broken Bow Road
Fort Collins, CO 80526
(970) 226-6050
www.centerforloss.com

THE
UNDERSTANDING
YOUR SUICIDE GRIEF

Support Group

GUIDE

STARTING AND LEADING
A BEREAVEMENT SUPPORT GROUP

[SECOND EDITION]

ALAN D. WOLFELT, PH.D.

Companion
PRESS

Fort Collins, Colorado
An imprint of the Center for Loss and Life Transition

First edition, ISBN 978-1-879651-60-9 © 2009 by Alan D. Wolfelt, Ph.D.

Second edition, ISBN 978-1-61722-339-6 © 2024 by Alan D. Wolfelt, Ph.D.

Companion Press is an imprint of the
Center for Loss and Life Transition
3735 Broken Bow Road
Fort Collins, Colorado 80526

Printed in the United States of America

30   29   28   27   26   25   24   6   5   4   3   2   1

ISBN: 978-1-61722-339-6

The *Understanding Your Suicide Grief* Series

SECOND EDITION

This book is designed for grief support group facilitator use along with *Understanding Your Suicide Grief, Second Edition* and *The Understanding Your Suicide Grief Journal, Second Edition*, also by Dr. Alan Wolfelt.

There is also a daily reader titled *365 Days of Understanding Your Grief* available. This text, while not tied specifically to suicide loss, makes an ideal supplemental support group text or participant graduation gift.

Contents

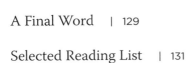

Introduction

IN GRATITUDE TO THE SUICIDE GRIEF
SUPPORT GROUP FACILITATOR

If you hope to support other people in their grief journeys and are planning to use this *Support Group Guide* in conjunction with the *Understanding Your Suicide Grief* book and journal (second editions), let me begin by thanking you.

Grief, often the most profound form of sorrow, demands the support and compassion of our fellow human beings. Since the beginning of time, people have come together in times of grief to help one another. Grief support groups provide an opportunity for this kind of care and support. Again, thank you for your efforts to help create a safe place to nurture suicide loss survivors. When you are privileged to witness the pain soften and hope emerge, you realize it is worth all your efforts.

Yes, starting and leading a grief support group is not only worth the effort, it is enriching and rewarding. My forty years of experience companioning people in grief have taught me that it is a true privilege to walk with and learn from my fellow travelers. They have taught me so much about individual and group support. Now, a vital part of the mission of my Center for Loss and Life Transition is to give back what I have learned.

The Medical Model of Bereavement Care

One important thing I have learned is that much of what I was taught about grief while I was earning my doctorate in psychology was too rooted in the medical model of caregiving. Like me, many mental health caregivers were trained in this model. They were taught that grief, like other psychological troubles, could be considered an illness that needs proper assessment and diagnosis and, with treatment, can be "cured."

I believe the limitations of our clinical, medical models are profound and far-reaching. Our modern understanding of grief all too often projects that for "successful" mourning to take place, the person must disengage from the person who died and, by all means "let go." We even have all sorts of books full of techniques on how to help others "let go" or reach "closure."

Our modern understanding of grief often urges people who are bereaved (which means "to be torn apart," "to have unique needs") to deny any form of continued relationship with the person who died. For many, the hallmark of so-called "pathological grief" has been the continued relationship mourners feel between themselves and those who have died.

Our modern understanding of grief all too often conveys that the end result of bereavement is a series of completed tasks, extinguished pain, and the establishment of new relationships. In attempting to make a science of grief, we have compartmentalized complex emotions with neat clinical labels.

Our modern understanding of grief all too often uses a "recovery" or "resolution" definition to suggest a return to "normalcy." Recovery, as understood by some, mourners and caregivers alike, is erroneously seen as an absolute, a perfect state of reestablishment.

Our modern understanding of grief for some is based on the model of crisis theory that purports that a person's life is in a state of homeostatic balance, then something comes along (like death) and knocks the person out of balance. Caregivers are taught intervention goals to reestablish the prior state of homeostasis. But there is a major problem with this theory—it doesn't work. Why? Because a person's life is changed forever by the death of someone loved.

Our modern understanding of grief all too often pathologizes others' experiences with disregard for cultural and personality differences. (For example, keening—making loud guttural, visceral noises of protest—is legitimized in some cultures and seen as abnormal in others. Better watch where you keen; you may be diagnosed with "Prolonged Grief Disorder.")

Our modern understanding of grief all too often lacks any appreciation for and attention to the spiritual nature of the grief journey. As thinkers such as Frankl, Fromm, and Jung noted years ago, and Hillman, more recently, academic psychology has been too interfaced with the natural sciences and laboratory methods of weighing, counting, and objective reporting. Some of us, often through no fault of our own but perhaps by the contamination of our formal training, have overlooked the fact that the journey into grief is a soul-based journey.

If you are a layperson who will be leading a suicide grief support group, you may also have been affected by the medical model of bereavement care. Have you absorbed our culture's judgments that it is wrong to cry in public, that the person who died wouldn't want us to be sad, that mourners need to find ways to "get over" their grief? These misconceptions are in part an outgrowth of the dominant (and harmful) medical model of bereavement care.

The Art of Companioning

The word "treat" comes from the Latin root word *tractare*, which means "to drag." If we combine that with the term "patient," we can really get into trouble. "Patient" means "passive long-term sufferer," so if we treat patients, we drag passive long-term sufferers. Doesn't sound very empowering to me.

Instead of the medical model of bereavement caregiving, I support a more soulful, holistic model of what it means to help someone in grief. I call it my "companioning" model of bereavement care.

The word "companion," when broken down into its original Latin roots, means "messmate": *com* for "with" and *pan* for "bread." Someone you would share a meal with, a friend, an equal. I have taken liberties with the noun "companion" and made it into the verb "companioning" because it so well captures the type of counseling relationship I support and advocate.

More specifically, for me...

- Companioning is about being present to another person's pain; it is not about taking away the pain.

- Companioning is about going to the wilderness of the soul with another human being; it is not about thinking you are responsible for finding the way out.

- Companioning is about honoring the spirit; it is not about focusing on the intellect.

- Companioning is about listening with the heart; it is not about analyzing with the head.

- Companioning is about bearing witness to the struggles of others; it is not about judging or directing these struggles.

- Companioning is about walking alongside; it is not about leading.

- Companioning is about discovering the gifts of sacred silence; it is not about filling up every moment with words.

- Companioning is about being still; it is not about frantic movement forward.

- Companioning is about respecting disorder and confusion; it is not about imposing order and logic.

- Companioning is about learning from others; it is not about teaching them.

- Companioning is about compassionate curiosity; it is not about expertise.

Yes, the grief journey requires contemplation and turning inward. In other words, it may include elements of depression, anxiety, and feelings of loss of control. It requires going to the wilderness. Quietness and emptiness invite the heart to observe signs of sacredness, to regain purpose, to rediscover love, to renew life! Searching for meaning and reasons to get one's feet out of bed, as well as understanding the pain of normal human loss, are not the domain of the medical model of bereavement care. Experience has taught me that it is the mysterious, spiritual dimension of grief that harbors the capacity to go on living until we, too, die.

I encourage you to hold the companioning philosophy of bereavement care in your heart as you support your group members.

The Myth of the Expert in Grief

There is a Buddhist teaching that says, "In the beginner's mind there are many possibilities; in the expert's mind there are few." Let's explore the consequences when others, such as your group members, think of you as an "expert."

In his lovely book *Improvisational Therapy*, Bradford P. Kenney writes brilliantly about the hazards of being considered an "expert" or "master" counselor:

> *You will find that it no longer matters what you say. Everything uttered will be contextualized as the voice of a master. A casual handshake will be taken as a trance induction. A belch becomes a brilliant intervention. The snoring in a nap becomes the voice of therapeutic wisdom.*
>
> *Avoid the political posturings of "mastery" and return to embracing and cultivating a beginner's mind. Maintain and respect ignorance. Speak to hear the surprise from your own voice.*

As you contemplate the risk of being an expert, listen to your own inner voice. What has your personal grief taught you about what helps people heal? What have grieving people taught you? What are your own personal strengths and limitations as a caregiver? Are you an open learner who is willing to be taught, or are you an expert who treats people like patients?

Many of you out there are not certified grief educators, counselors, or therapists. That doesn't mean, however, you aren't resourceful, talented, compassionate people who can help people heal in grief. I encourage you to continue to grow and learn while at the same time not striving to be an expert. Continual development and openness to learning new tools and ways of being are essential for all of us.

As caregivers to people in grief, I believe we would be well-served to discover our own unique styles and gifts. It was humanist thinker and educational theorist Arthur Wright Combs who years ago introduced the concept of "self-as-instrument" to the counseling literature.

He warned against the strict adherence to a particular model or school of counseling and essentially urged caregivers to discover their unique gifts and make use of them. He warned that we shouldn't become counselors cloned in the image of others but instead strive to awaken, cultivate, and nurture imagination and creativity in ourselves, in our colleagues, and in our clients.

I believe that counseling people in grief—as well as leading grief support groups—is more of an art than a science. An artist fully embraces their personal strengths and limitations to develop a unique style that becomes a self-portrait as a counselor and as a human being.

Using the *Support Group Guide*

This *Support Group Guide* is to help you get started with and facilitate your suicide grief support group. The contents cover a variety of important topics, from planning group meetings to responding to potential problems in the group and evaluating your group's progress. I hope you will also find the twelve-session group meeting plan using *Understanding Your Suicide Grief* to be of help to you as you reach out to minister to those in need of a meaningful group experience.

Please note that to use the twelve-session plan, each of your group members will need to have a copy of both *Understanding Your Suicide Grief—Second Edition* and *The Understanding Your Suicide Grief Journal—Second Edition*. It's important that everyone use the second editions of all three books because content has been revised and added since the first edition, and page number references and journal questions have also been updated. They are available through the Center for Loss bookstore at centerforloss.com. Information related to a Suicide Grief Support Group Start-Up package is also available at centerforloss.com.

You and the grieving people you will go on to help will be held in my thoughts and prayers. Grieving people need to know they are not alone—that there are safe places and kind and loving people willing to help them. Even in the wilderness of grief, they can reach out and find comfort and support. Most of all, they can discover there is hope for tomorrow. These are the critical ingredients for healing.

Best wishes as you companion those who mourn.

Sincerely,

Alan D. Wolfelt, Ph.D.
Director, Center for Loss and Life Transition

The Role of
Support Groups

In her book, *A Mother's Story*, Gloria Vanderbilt beautifully makes the following observation: "As strangers, we enter the room of this support group. But later, sitting in a circle, we were not strangers, not even friends. We were a family, one that does not judge, for pain has stripped us bare. Ah, yes, we knew each other well."

There is no doubt that support groups are an appropriate and effective way to help many suicide loss survivors heal. Because they offer a safe place for people to do the work of mourning, support groups encourage participants to reconcile their losses and go on to find continued meaning in life and living. Attending a suicide grief support group facilitated by a skilled leader often brings comfort and understanding beyond many people's expectations.

Support groups help grieving people by:

- introducing them to others who have had similar experiences, thoughts, and feelings.

- countering the sense of isolation that many experience in our shame-based, mourning-avoidant culture.

- providing emotional, physical, and spiritual support in a safe, nonjudgmental environment.

- allowing them to explore their many thoughts and feelings about grief in a way that helps them be compassionate with themselves.

- encouraging members to not only receive support and understanding for themselves but also to provide the same to others.

"The quality and quantity of understanding support you get during your work of mourning will have a major influence on your capacity to heal. You cannot—nor should you try to—do this alone. Drawing on the experiences and encouragement of friends, fellow grievers, and professional counselors is not a weakness but a healthy human need."

Alan Wolfelt,
Understanding Your Grief

- offering opportunities to learn new ways of approaching problems (e.g., the friend or in-law who lacks an understanding of the need to mourn and pushes a support group participant to "get over it").

- showing them they can trust their fellow human beings and bond again in what for many in grief feels like an unsafe, uncaring world.

- giving them a forum to search for meaning in life and death.

- providing a supportive environment that can reawaken their zest for life and give them hope for healing.

In short, as group members both give and receive help, they feel less helpless and are able to discover continued meaning in life. Feeling understood by others brings down barriers between the grieving person and the world outside. This process of being understood is central to being compassionate with oneself as a bereaved person. The more people are compassionate to the bereaved from the outside in, the more the bereaved are capable of being self-compassionate from the inside out.

Our mourning-avoidant culture often forces grieving people to withdraw from insensitive friends and family or to adopt ways of avoiding the painful but necessary work of mourning. Support groups, which instead foster the experience of trusting and being trusted, can do wonders in meeting the needs of bereaved people. In an effective suicide grief support group, members can achieve a balance between giving and receiving, between independence and an appropriate, self-sustaining interdependence. The group provides a safe harbor where hurting people can pull in, anchor while the wind still blows them around, and search for safe ground on which to go on living. As a potential leader of such a group, you have the honor of accompanying people during this time.

The Nuts and Bolts

Starting a suicide grief support group can take a lot of time and energy. In fact, I have seen many people decide *not* to start groups simply because they foresaw too many roadblocks and details to attend to. But let me tell you a little secret: even though you will be group leader, you needn't do everything yourself! Instead, round up other interested community members to help you with the start-up activities. A committee of compassionate caregivers and grieving people can share the workload and even more important, bring a variety of valuable ideas to the process.

As you complete them, check off the following start-up tasks:

☐ Performing a needs assessment

Before your commendable enthusiasm causes you to plunge headlong into running your support group, step back and formally assess the interest in and need for grief support groups in your community. Questions to address include: What kind of grief support groups already exist in this community? Are there any specific suicide grief support groups? What has been the history and success of these groups? What have the leaders of these groups learned about what works and what doesn't? If a new group is started, are there enough people interested in being group members? Who else is willing to commit time and effort to make this group successful?

Deciding on a group format

What kind of support group will you provide? Many support groups combine education with support and may be facilitated by either a trained layperson or a professional counselor. Self-help groups (which may or may not be affiliated with a national organization, such as the American Foundation for Suicide Prevention) are led by grieving people who have already worked toward reconciliation of the death of someone loved. (*The Understanding Your Suicide Grief* model relates to both support groups and self-help groups.) Therapy support groups are led by professional therapists and are limited to a small number of members. Social support groups are usually intended for people who have already worked toward reconciliation of the death of someone loved but who would benefit from social contact with people who share their experiences.

You also must decide who will join your group. Will the group be homogeneous—made up of people who have experienced a specific type of loss (in this situation, suicide)—or will their common bond simply be that each group member has had someone loved die? In homogeneous groups, the similarity of losses often creates a tremendous bond for members and makes relating to one another very easy. I have found this to be particular true with suicide grief support groups. However, depending on the size of your community, you may or may not be able to achieve this homogeneity. In small communities, you may need to intermix mourners with different loss histories, but I do not recommend combining death loss with other types of loss (such as divorce, illness, etc.) in your support group. The main thing to avoid is having someone feel so different from other group members that they feel alone and isolated.

RUNNING A GRIEF SUPPORT GROUP ONLINE

While my preference is in-person suicide grief support groups, the reality is that the COVID pandemic forced many organizations to create online offerings. In the wake of the pandemic, some of the groups have continued online. They allow people who travel or live farther away to participate. Some group members may also feel more comfortable participating from their own homes than traveling.

What follows are some general tips for providing groups online:

- **Get comfortable with the technology.** The leader must know how to run the online platform well and be comfortable with all its features, such as the waiting room, screen sharing, and break-out groups.

- **Find ways to manage online challenges.** Can participants turn off their cameras? What if background noises are distracting? Is it OK to step away from the meeting for a minute? How will you handle confidentiality if others in the members' homes can hear or see what's going on? The group leader must be prepared to create and enforce a few groundrules about online etiquette and help educate less tech-savvy members about how to use the tools.

- **Make use of co-facilitators.** It can be challenging for an individual facilitator to coordinate the technology demands as well as the interpersonal elements of the group dynamics. Having a co-facilitator can help overcome these natural challenges. One facilitator can focus on the group process, while the other can provide the necessary technological support.

- **Consider group size.** An appropriate group is small enough for people to participate and meet the need for mutual support. A group too big, especially online, runs the risk of participants feeling overwhelmed or tuning out. Should your group participation numbers get too high, consider making use of break-out rooms to divide into smaller groups led by co-facilitators. This allows everyone who participates the chance to give and receive the support they need and deserve.

- **Routine is even more important.** The structure of each meeting may be even more important online. Ask people to "arrive" on time, then use an opening ritual of some kind. Consider "closing the door" after the opening ritual, so that people can't join midway through the meeting. Sequence each meeting in a predictable way.
- **Part online, part in-person may be a nice combination.** This type of hybrid approach would allow groups to continue to meet in bad weather or when members are feeling a bit under the weather or are traveling.

If you are new to offering online suicide grief support groups, I encourage you to find experienced mentors who can be available to you as any questions or concerns might arise. It would also be helpful to plan to debrief with mentors following each meeting.

Finally, will this be an in-person or an online grief support group? During the COVID pandemic, virtual grief support groups burgeoned. This book is primarily intended for use with in-person grief support groups, but the lesson plans can be adapted for online facilitation. Keeping an online group small— I suggest no more than six to eight members—would help keep it intimate and better mimic the interpersonal benefits of an in-person group.

☐ Finding a compatible co-leader

While you may choose to lead this support group by yourself, there are a number of good reasons to have a co-leader. First, leading a support group can be a lot of work. Having two people to plan meetings and lead discussions splits the burden. It also gives you someone to bounce ideas off and debrief with after meetings. If there is a problem in the group, your co-leader can help troubleshoot it. If you are sick or traveling one week, instead of canceling the meeting as you would have to do if you were the only leader, your co-leader can probably manage without you. Just be certain to find someone with a similar philosophy about grief and a compatible personality.

Finding and preparing a meeting place

Obviously, you hope to find a comfortable, safe place to hold your group meetings. Public buildings such as libraries, schools, churches, and community centers sometimes provide rooms for nonprofit use free-of-charge. Try to select a room appropriate for creating a supportive atmosphere, neither too large nor too small and preferably distraction-free. A room away from heavy traffic areas is best. Also, pay attention to both the height of the ceiling and the lighting. Very high ceilings often make for a lack of intimacy. Lamps that provide soft lighting are preferable to bright overhead lights. A large whiteboard is handy for many of the meeting activities. You may also want to consider using your phone and a portable Bluetooth speaker to play soft, appropriate music in the background to start and/or conclude your meetings. Be sensitive to how the music you might play could be an activating experience for some group members.

☐ Setting the number of participants

The maximum number of support group members you permit will be related to the kind and quality of interaction you desire. When groups get too large, the sense of safety and freedom to be verbally expressive diminishes for many people. For involved interaction, try to limit your group to no more than twelve members (possibly fewer if you're meeting online or if you don't have a co-leader).

Establishing the structure of the group

You must also determine the structure of the support group. Will it be "open-ended," meaning that group members come and go depending on their needs? Or will it be "closed-ended," meaning that the group will start on a certain date and meet for a specific number of days or weeks? In my experience, members feel more comfortable knowing specifically when the group will begin and when it will end. What's more, I'm a proponent of closed-ended groups because when everyone starts and stops at the same time, members share a powerful experience and the group goes through the developmental phases we'll be talking about later in this resource. The model outlined in this resource is for a close-ended suicide grief support group.

☐ Determining length and frequency of meetings

My experience suggests that grief support groups for adults work best when each meeting runs ninety minutes to two hours. Some of your length considerations will have to do with the number of participants you have; to give everyone a chance to talk, larger groups demand longer meetings.

Some groups meet weekly, some biweekly, some monthly. Be creative in determining which length and frequency will work best for your unique group and your unique community. The meeting plans outlined in this book are intended for a group that meets weekly for twelve consecutive weeks.

☐ Prescreening group members

Not every grieving person makes a good support group member. People with extensive complications of their grief journey or histories of serious emotional or mental health challenges are generally better helped by individual counseling. This will be a judgment call on your part, so don't punish yourself if you occasionally admit someone to a group whom you later determine would be better served elsewhere.

How do you prescreen? If time permits, I recommend you conduct brief, one-on-one meetings with potential group members before the group begins, in person or over the phone. Another alternative is to see how the first group meeting goes *then* privately screen out those whose grief journeys make them more likely candidates for individual counseling. With the latter method, however, you risk alienating group members from the start if one among them behaves inappropriately during the first meeting. Therefore, I do not recommend making use of this method.

While screening, you may also want to pay attention to the recency of the loss. Some grievers are drawn to joining a support group immediately, while others feel too psychically numb to engage until some months or even years have passed. It's OK to have a mixture in your group. Both responses are normal, and it's important not to shame anyone who has had a very recent loss and wants to participate. Sometimes suicide loss survivors desperately need the lifeline a grief group can provide. If a new mourner joins the group and is overwhelmed by the experience, however, it may be appropriate to suggest to them that they sit out this group and return the next time the group is offered. In the meantime, individual counseling may offer them just the support they need. It's also OK for support group members experiencing significant shock and numbness during the first session to repeat the entire group experience a second time.

Here are some suggested prescreening questions:

- Who in your life has died by suicide?

- When was the loss?

- Have you experienced other significant losses in the past?

- Can you please share a little about the support you have been receiving so far from others in your life?

- Are you seeing a counselor? If so, have you spoken to your counselor about attending the group?

- Have you participated in any other support groups?

- Do you or have you had any previous experiences with depression, anxiety, or other mental health issues? Are you taking medication for any physical or emotional difficulties?

- Is there anything else I might need to know about your interest in and capacity to participate in this support group?

WHAT IF I MISS?

What to do if you find a group member's needs are too great

Even if you've done a good job prescreening group members, once in a while it will turn out that a participant isn't suited to your group after all. If this has happened to you, go easy on yourself! I've been prescreening and doing grief groups for many years, and I "miss" sometimes, too.

When a participant has serious complications in their grief and the group attempts to help with all of them, this can result in the group spending the bulk of its time on one member's needs to the exclusion of everyone else. I have witnessed grief groups that attempt to carry a load of care that is so large it destroys the entire group.

If you discover there is a mismatch between a participant's needs and the group's ability to help, you have an ethical responsibility to refer the person to other sources of support and care. Don't try to include someone in your group who really needs individual, professional counseling. When a group leader tries to provide individual counseling in the group setting, it serves neither the person experiencing complicated grief nor the rest of the group. Often the participant knows on some level they need more help and are grateful for your referral. Be sure you're knowledgeable about your community's grief-informed counselors and their areas of specialty. Whenever possible, you will want to make referrals to caregivers trained in companioning mourners with complicated grief.

☐ Creating group groundrules

Through appropriately prescreening participants and establishing group groundrules, you can create a safe place for people to mourn. Groundrules are also important to your role as a leader. For example, should someone begin to verbally dominate the group, you can intervene by pointing out a groundrule that ensures members will have equal time to express themselves. I suggest you distribute copies of your group's groundrules to all participants during the first session. You might also want to post them in your meeting room.

See the sample groundrules on the next page for suggestions.

SAMPLE SUICIDE GRIEF SUPPORT GROUP GROUNDRULES

1. Each person's grief is unique. While you may share some commonalities in your experiences, no two of you are exactly alike, and no two losses are exactly alike. Consequently, respect and accept both what you have in common with others and what is unique to each of you.

2. Grief is not a disease, and no quick fix exists for what you are feeling. Don't set a specific timetable for how long it should take you or others to heal.

3. You are encouaraged to talk about your grief. However, if someone in the group decides to listen without sharing, please respect their preference.

4. You are encouraged to refrain from detailed sharing that may be activating for fellow group members. This includes detailed description of specific methods, describing the location of the death in minute detail, and overly discussing information about discovering the body of the person that died.

5. There is a difference between actively listening to what another person is saying and expressing your own thoughts and feelings. Make every effort not to interrupt when someone else is speaking.

7. Thoughts, feelings, and experiences shared in this group will stay in this group. Respect others' right to confidentiality. Do not use names of fellow participants in discussions outside the group or share identifying details.

7. Allow each person equal time to express themself so a few people don't monopolize the group's time.

8. Attend each group meeting and be on time. If you decide to leave the group before this series of meetings is completed, be willing to discuss your decision with the group leaders.

9. Avoid giving advice unless it is specifically requested by a group member. If advice is not solicited, don't give it. If a group member asks, then it's OK to share ideas that helped you in a similar situation. Remember that this group is for support, not therapy.

10. Create an atmosphere of willing, invited sharing. If you feel pressured to talk but don't want to, say so. Your right to quiet contemplation will be respected by the group.

☐ Publicizing your group

There are a number of strategies you can use to publicize a support group. Try any or all of the following:

WORD-OF-MOUTH

Share information about the group with everyone you can, and ask that they in turn share it with others.

DIRECT COMMUNICATION WITH MEDICAL/MENTAL HEALTH PROFESSIONALS

Start by identifying the professionals and laypeople in your community who work with grieving people, such as counselors and staff at hospices, funeral homes, and places of worship. In addition to speaking personally to these people (a brief face-to-face or phone conversation will suffice), you can ask if they'll allow you to place posters, flyers, and/or brochures about your support group in their offices.

EMAIL LIST

You might also want to compile an email list comprised of area counselors, funeral directors, hospice directors, religious leaders, and more.

LOCAL MEDIA

Many communities have a newspaper that provides a community calendar that will announce your group, provide a brief description about it, and explain how to contact the leader responsible for additional information and prescreening. The newspaper editor may even be willing to feature an article about the group, especially if it is a new group in the community.

Radio and TV stations may also have the equivalent of a community calendar to feature the group. If your organization has a media specialist, a press release could be written and sent to local newspapers, radio, and TV stations.

POSTERS, FLYERS, AND BROCHURES

Posters, flyers, and brochures are other effective ways of marketing a suicide grief support group. Logical places to post them include hospices, funeral homes, hospitals, and even coffee shops and grocery stores.

THE INTERNET

Last but certainly not least is the internet. If your group is sponsored by a community organization, you may want to create a webpage about the support group on the agency's website. Or you can create a dedicated website just for the group by using a simple, free tool such as Weebly or Wix. If possible, provide a phone number or email address so interested community members can contact the group leader, co-leader, or administrative contact, or provide a form for people to type in their contact information so someone can reach out to them.

Social media can also be an excellent tool for promoting a grief support group. You can create a Facebook page or Instagram account for the group and use it to promote grief awareness as well as help get out the word about your group.

Leadership
Roles

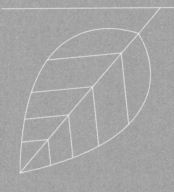

A suicide grief support group leader serves the group by enabling members to achieve the purpose of the support group. That purpose is generally to create a safe, supportive place for people to do the work of mourning in a way that helps them begin to move toward reconciling the loss and finding continued meaning in life and living.

Obviously, your specific support group may have varying purposes and goals that guide its existence. No matter the goals, however, the group leader's responsibilities remain largely the same. They are responsible for assisting the group in:

- determining the group's purpose
- outlining the group's structure and length
- prescreening potential members
- clarifying expectations and assisting in the development of group groundrules
- organizing details

Now let's explore some of the specific tasks that will probably be part of your support group leader job description. Again, keep in mind that every group has its own unique requirements.

ARTICULATING A GUIDING PHILOSOPHY:
Identifying the basic tenets (theoretical orientation) that guide your way of being as facilitator and providing a rationale for any skills or techniques you make use of in group.

PLANNING AND LEADING GROUP MEETINGS:
Preparing for, organizing, and facilitating the group meetings.

LISTENING:
To model effective listening, you must really hear and allow participants to teach you and each other what they are thinking and feeling.

UNDERSTANDING AND FACILITATING GROUP PROCESS:
Having knowledge of and being skilled in facilitating group process. I cannot emphasize enough the importance of leaders getting some

fundamental training, not only in the grief process, but also in group process.

MODELING OPENNESS AND CARING:
Providing a role model by being warm, caring, and empathetic and by consciously seeking ways to help the group achieve its purpose.

REMAINING FLEXIBLE:
Staying aware of the need to modify group activities to fit the unique needs of a specific group or a specific meeting.

BEING RESPONSIVE TO CONFLICTS AND PROBLEMS THAT EVOLVE:
Guiding the group through difficulties that may come up and responding appropriately to destructive behavior in the group.

ACTIVATING EXPERIENCES:
Providing opportunities for group members to debrief any activating experiences that might occur.

LEARNING ABOUT EFFECTIVE GROUP LEADERSHIP ROLES:
Participating in training opportunities that allow you to assess current skills and develop new ones.

BASIC NEEDS OF GRIEF SUPPORT GROUP MEMBERS

- Each member must understand the purpose of the group.
- Each member must feel a sense of belonging and acceptance.
- Each member must feel understood.
- Each member must be aware of and respectful of the groundrules.
- Each member must feel encouraged to be an active participant in the group while also feeling respected if they choose to remain quiet.
- Each member must be able to see the faces of all other members during group meetings to effectively communicate (so arrange the seating appropriately).

FOLLOWING UP WITH MEMBERS OUTSIDE OF THE GROUP:
Some members will appreciate opportunities to talk individually, while others may need referral for a counseling relationship. It is very important to recognize that some members will have activating experiences that require the need to debrief with a group leader. It is also the group leader's responsibility to help members transfer learning in the group to daily life.

EVALUATING GROUP PROGRESS:
Monitoring the group's capacity to achieve its purpose and make any changes to improve this process.

If you don't already have one, I encourage you to write out a job description for your suicide grief support group facilitators. This will help both you and any organization you represent: 1) clarify the details of your role as a group leader; 2) help you get started in your new role; and 3) avoid unstated expectations. A seat-of-the-pants orientation to group facilitation is dangerous and minimizes your responsibility as a leader. With appropriate preparation and training, your leadership role will be both satisfying and enjoyable.

Grief support group leader qualities

One of the foundations of good suicide grief support group leadership is communication. To be helpful to your group members, you must communicate with them effectively and make them feel cared for.

We all have probably known people we would call "natural helpers." Actually, the helping skills that seem so natural to them are more likely characteristics and qualities they have learned and developed over time. The most important quality is empathy, but there are others described below, as well. You, too, have the capacity to learn, enhance, and make use of these helping qualities.

Empathy
Empathy is the ability to perceive another's experience and then— this is the key—communicate that perception back to the person.

As a support group leader, I listen to you, and though I cannot experience what you are experiencing, I begin to have a deep appreciation for the essence of what you are describing.

Perhaps the most vital part of this characteristic is the ability to convey accurate empathy. Empathetic responsiveness requires the ability to go beyond factual detail and to become involved in the other person's feeling world, but always with the "as-if-I-were-in-their-shoes" quality of taking another's role without personally experiencing what the other person experiences. To have empathy for another person does not constitute the direct expression of one's own feelings but rather focuses exclusively on the feelings expressed by another, thereby conveying an understanding of them.

You know that empathy has been communicated when your group members feel that you "understand." As you know, to say simply, "I understand how you feel" is not enough. The response goes beyond the "I understand how you feel" level to the "You really are feeling a sense of loss" level. In other words, empathy is communicated both verbally and nonverbally by embracing the person's experience at the emotional level.

Respect

Respect is your ability to communicate your belief that everyone has inherent value as well as the capacity and right to choose and make decisions. Respect requires a non-possessive caring for and affirmation of another person, respecting another's right to be who and what they are. This quality involves a receptive attitude that embraces the other person's feelings, opinions, and uniqueness— even those radically different from your own.

The dimension of respect is communicated when support group members feel they have been allowed to give input without being pressured and when their opinions have been considered important. Remembering what the person has said, demonstrating sensitivity and courtesy, and showing respect for the person's feelings and beliefs is the essence of communicating respect.

Warmth and Caring

The warm and caring support group leader cultivates a sense of personal closeness, as opposed to professional distance, with group members. Showing you are warm and caring is particularly helpful in the early phases of building a helping relationship. Warmth is communicated with posture, body language, affect, facial expression, and other nonverbal cues as well as verbal cues such as tone of voice, word choice, and more.

Warmth is a very powerful dimension in the helping process. In fact, when a discrepancy exists between verbal and nonverbal behavior, people almost always believe the nonverbal. A person's nonverbal behavior seldom lies. Consequently, a person who has excellent verbal communication skills but lacks "warm" nonverbal behavior would more than likely be perceived by group members as unhelpful, indifferent, cold, or uncaring.

Genuineness

Genuineness is the ability to present oneself sincerely. As a support group leader, this is your ability to be freely yourself—without phoniness, roleplaying, or defensiveness. It's when your words and behaviors match your inner feelings.

The dimension of genuineness involves disclosing how you feel about an issue. One important caveat: try not to tell group members how you feel too early because your opinion may interfere with their ability to open up and express their own unique and equally valid thoughts and feelings. Genuineness is essential, but timing is important. You can earn the right to be genuine with others through first developing the relationship.

Suicide grief support group leader skills

In addition to the innate and learned qualities described above, there are a number of skills for you to learn and practice if you are to be the most effective suicide grief support group leader you can be. It is my bias that the skills or techniques that are most useful evolve out of the work of the members and are specific to the unique meeting. In other words, at any given meeting the members will teach you what skills they need that day.

Instead of using skills to make something happen, use them to elaborate on what is already happening. In other words, *skills are means, not ends.* In using skills, you always want to keep clearly in mind the primary purposes of your group. The use of specific skills should also be dependent on the population you are working with (support versus therapy group) and the unique personality of individual group members (e.g., some members dislike confrontation while others can tolerate it or may even seek it out). Of course, cultural influences must also be respected whenever you use specific skills.

It's very important that you find an experienced mentor to help you learn these skills and provide supervision both early on and throughout the unfolding of your group. I suggest that your experienced mentor meet with you a minimum of three times throughout the twelve sessions outlined in this model. In addition, if you have not already, plan to attend a training on group process from an experienced group facilitator. What you are reading here is just an introductory summary. You will need a mentor to help you develop these group skills over time.

SKILL	GROUP MEMBERS' RESPONSE	EXPECTED OUTCOME
ATTENDING: Listening, giving attention to each person.	Communicates that you are listening; makes them aware of your concern.	Helps build the relationship; enhances trust.
PARAPHRASING: Restating the person's basic message in similar, but fewer, words.	Feels supported and really heard, accepted.	Creates clearer self-perception.
CLARIFYING: Bringing vague content into clearer focus.	Clears up vague and confusing messages.	Clearer statements and increased understanding.
PERCEPTION CHECKING: Asks for feedback about accuracy of your listening: "Is that right?"	Allows person to feel accurately understood.	Quickly clears up any confusing communication.
LEADING: Anticipating where the member is going and offering an encouraging remark.	Allows members to explore in a direction they need to discuss.	Encourages members to be responsible for direction of the interaction.
ENCOURAGING DESCRIPTION AND EXPLORATION: Allowing for more depth in communication or reflection on experiences: "What was that like for you when Mary said that to you?"	Elaborates on their experience: "I was angry."	Members move to greater depth of experience (must be well-timed and well-paced).
PROVIDING INFORMATION: "The purpose of this activity is..."	Assists in understanding of the "why" of doing an activity.	Leaders and members increase trust with each other when they know the why of the activities.

SKILL	GROUP MEMBERS' RESPONSE	EXPECTED OUTCOME
FOCUSING: Identifying a single topic to concentrate on: "Maybe we could talk more about your friend's response to your sadness."	Channels thinking and feeling about a topic of individual and group concern.	Increases members' understanding of one area before moving to another topic.
ALLOWING FOR CONSENSUAL VALIDATION: Seeking a mutual (group) understanding of what is being said. "I've seen a lot of progress in you in that area. I wonder what other changes group members have seen in you?"	Invites group members to share observations of a particular member and offer support and encouragement.	Individual members learn how others perceive them. Empowers members who offer supportive observations.
REFLECTING FEELINGS: Expressing in fresh words the essential feelings, stated or implied, of the person.	Helps members bring feelings into clearer awareness.	Gives members the message that you and the group accept their feelings.
MAKING OBSERVATIONS: "John, I notice you seem much more at peace with yourself than when we first began to meet as a group."	Member has something to respond to: "Yes, I am more at peace with myself."	Leader and members place attention on significant observations and can then explore them.
PROVIDING ACKNOWLEDGMENT: "Sue, you look like you really relate to that. Does that fit with your experience?"	Members feels acknowledged and valued.	Leader models the need to acknowledge nonverbal forms of communication.

SKILL	GROUP MEMBERS' RESPONSE	EXPECTED OUTCOME
NONJUDGMENTAL ACCEPTANCE: "Bill, it sounds like you are not sure you want to be here." (Tone is important.)	Feels understood without fear of being attacked.	Members learn any thought can be expressed and talked about in the group.
ENCOURAGING COMPARISON: Asking members to contrast their experiences with others in the group. "How have others of us responded to this problem?"	Members share their ways of responding to a similar situation.	Greater insight of all members results from shared commonalities and differences. Learn alternative responses to problems, concerns.
SUPPORTIVE CONFRONTATION: A leader response that helps a member explore what they want to avoid: "I hear you say you have no support, yet you have given me a number of examples of how people around you give you support."	Assists the member in achievement of congruency (what they say and how they behave correspond).	Creates a clearer self-perception and allows for greater self-exploration.
SUMMARIZING: A method of tying together several ideas and feelings at the end of a discussion or group session: "As a group, we seemed to discuss several areas of concern today..."	Helps leaders and members recall and affirm important learnings or self-discoveries, provides a sense of progress toward healing.	Results in enhanced understanding and self-awareness; results in better understanding of group process.

Building trust

As a responsible leader, you will need to work on not only the qualities and skills I've set forth in this chapter, you will also need to be sensitive to the need to consciously create conditions for mutual trust to grow within the group.

One important way is by facilitating the honoring of stories. It is through the sharing of personal experiences that group members will do the work of mourning in your group, and as they do this work, mutual empathy and trust naturally build over time. The more time you allow for sharing stories, the deeper the expression of feelings will be, and the more rapidly your group's trust, relationships, and sense of community will grow.

Naturally, as trust builds, members feel more comfortable expressing a multitude of thoughts and feelings. In the beginning, participants tend to express safer or more expected feelings, but as trust increases, they often share more vulnerable feelings such as fear, helplessness, and anger. Obviously, as participants take greater risks in expressing themselves and continue to experience compassion and empathy from other members as well as you, the leader, community grows.

Do remember that as you lead grief groups in honoring stories, personal sharing may be difficult for some members. Effective leadership means never forcing participation but encouraging and supporting it.

You also build trust by providing a safe place for the open, genuine expression of grief (mourning). To create an atmosphere for authentic mourning, encourage and support group members when they respond in compassionate ways to one another. As the group members witness the support in action from you and fellow members, they will come to realize that this group is a place in which they can honestly express what is going on with their grief.

Model for participants that it is not their responsibility to solve each other's problems but instead to support one another as they encounter the wilderness of grief. As participants realize they can express their grief without others giving unsolicited advice, they are more likely to trust each other and the group process.

And finally, to maintain trust, don't hesitate to revisit group groundrules when necessary. This is particularly true when it comes to activating experiences. You will need to stay alert for members that may over share details (method, location, discovery of body) that result in activating experiences for other group members as well as you as a leader. When this does happen (and it sometimes does), use your leadership skills to provide appropriate containment. This is also a natural time to revisit the groundrules related to this topic, and supportively emphasizing the importance of it.

The other important groundrule that helps build trust is the one specific to confidentiality. Do not hesitate to revisit the importance of this from time to time. Without confidentiality in a suicide grief support group, you have no trust.

Suggestions for leading discussions

As group leader, your role is to facilitate—which literally means to "make easier"— purposeful discussion about the grief journeys of group members. This is a task that will require some planning and forethought on your part. Consider the following suggestions:

PLAN EACH SESSION

Write down your goals and expectations for each group meeting. For example, your objective in the first session may simply be to get to know each other. How will you accomplish this? In addition to letting members tell their stories, you may plan one or two group activities. You might also use music and appropriate readings as prompts for group discussion.

HAVE A ROUTINE

Especially when they're feeling vulnerable, people like the comfort of a routine. You might, for example, open each session with a short reading that you or another member has brought. Try to start each meeting slowly; participants may need a few minutes to settle in and prepare themselves before they can befriend their pain.

REMEMBER YOU'RE LEADING
Allow yourself to be a contributing member of the group, especially if you're a layperson and one reason you started the group was to help yourself heal. However, don't forget your role and responsibilities as group leader.

BE SENSITIVE TO DIFFERENCES AMONG MEMBERS
As group leader, you are probably an outgoing person who feels comfortable sharing experiences in a group setting. Not all members will be so forthcoming. Don't force people to talk unless they're ready. On the other hand, you'll also need to be on the watch for the member who likes to talk too much and monopolizes the group's time.

A word of caution: there is a fine line between strong group leadership and strong-arming your group. While members will

---

SUPPORT GROUP RED FLAGS
Indications that trust may be lacking in a grief support group

The following red flags suggest that your group members haven't built enough mutual trust to make the group effective:

- A general unwillingness among members to share and contribute
- Long-winded expressions by only a few members
- A tendency for members to focus on others instead of themselves
- A member that has a desire to create activating experiences for themself and fellow members
- A belief by some members that the group cannot help them

Can you think of any other signs that trust is lacking?

appreciate your nurturing leadership, they will not appreciate too tight a rein on the group's interaction. (Always keep in mind what I said about "companioning" in the Introduction to this text. You must try to be both a companion and a leader at once!) Sometimes that means letting the group dynamic dictate what will happen next. Other times your gentle firmness will be welcomed as you guide the group in discussion.

Defining your leadership style

What kind of leader are you? Are you gregarious? Assertive? Calm? Leaders I have found most effective in suicide grief support groups lead unobtrusively but firmly. That is, they are warm and responsive at the same time they make others feel comfortable that someone is in charge.

Two more important qualities in an effective group leader are: 1) flexibility; and 2) the ability to share authority. Being flexible is important because some meetings—especially as the group evolves—will naturally flow without much direction from you. That means that sometimes your meeting plans, no matter how well conceived, should be tossed out the window if the group dynamic takes everyone in a different direction. A good leader is never rigid.

The ability and willingness to share your role as leader is also very important. As the group evolves, one or two members will sometimes step forward as unofficial co-leaders. This is about letting someone else lead a particular discussion or choose a particular reading. More important, though, it means letting the group dynamic—not your meeting plan—dictate the flow of each session when that dynamic is healthy and healing. The trick, of course, is to intervene and redirect when the dynamic is not healthy.

For more information on counseling skills and techniques, you may also want to look into my book *Counseling Skills for Companioning the Mourner: The Fundamentals of Effective Grief Counseling.*

The Support Group's Developmental Phases

Why is it important to understand that suicide grief support groups go through developmental phases? Because knowledge of these phases allows you to both respect and nurture the natural unfolding of the group's development. For example, if you were to expect in-depth self-disclosure of all members at the first meeting, you would not be respecting the reality that this kind of sharing generally does not happen until group trust has been established over time.

Groups tend to develop in spiraling stages. This means that mourning needs such as the telling of the story tend to be met again and again but at progressively deeper levels of vulnerability and meaning. Of course, individual group members and group dynamics have a vital influence on the process of group development, so the outline that follows is very theoretical.

PHASE ONE:
Warm-up and establishing of group purpose and limits

In the beginning of a support group, you can anticipate some normal anxiety about the general uncertainty of "what will happen here." Group members may be questioning their capacity to tolerate their own and others' pain. So, be aware that many group members will attend with a certain amount of hesitancy as well as questions about whether or not they should even be there.

Among the questions that may go through their minds during this phase: Who else is in this group? How does their loss relate to mine? Will they understand me or judge me? Will I feel comfortable with these people? What will we talk about? Are there certain expectations the group will have of me? Will the leader make it safe for me to just be who I am? Will I have to talk, even if at times I don't want to? Can I trust these people?

Behaviorally, members will tend to reflect their unique personalities. Some will be more expressive, while others may be silent and withdrawn. This initial period of getting to know each other is critical for what will or will not follow.

The leader plays a critical role in making it safe during this initial phase of the group's development. Here the primary leadership roles include:

- clarifying the purpose of the group.
- gently encouraging each member to tell their story (staying alert for any sharing that causes activating experiences).
- assisting in the creation of groundrules for the group.
- modeling listening and helping everyone feel as if they belong.
- facilitating details such as time of meetings, homework, etc.

PHASE TWO:
Tentative self-disclosure and exploring group boundaries

This is the phase where members begin to learn what is expected to happen in the group. Every group has expectations (spoken or unspoken) about what will happen in the group meeting. Essentially, members are learning how to be participating members of the support group.

At this stage members begin to see themselves as part of a group and disclose more about themselves. Often this self-disclosure is rather tentative. It's as if the group is exploring whether it's safe to move to a deeper level of vulnerability.

Differences in interpersonal styles and ways of coping with grief become more apparent during this phase, particularly among members who are more independent and take-charge-oriented with their grief journeys. Different group memebers may begin to display their behavioral styles of relating to the group.

Through increasing self-disclosure and the exploring of group norms and boundaries, members begin to learn more about each other, the leader, and themselves. During this phase the primary leadership roles include:

- continuing to model listening, openness, and caring.
- continuing to clarify member expectations of the group.
- reminding members of the groundrules established during the first meeting.
- providing the group's structure and facilitating any activities or homework to be discussed.
- being responsive to conflicts and problems that might evolve.

PHASE THREE:

In-depth self-exploration and encountering the pain of grief

As the group grows and develops, a subtle but important movement takes place. The group begins to move away from the initial discovery of the "why" of the group and toward an increasing involvement in the work of mourning. In this phase, the group has shifted from second to third gear and is beginning to develop group trust at a deeper level. A natural insider/outsider feeling often begins to develop, and certain members may begin to express how important the group is to them. Now the group is feeling good about itself, and members look forward to each meeting.

Informal co-leaders may begin to emerge; try not to let this pose a threat to the group or your leadership. A higher rate of interpersonal self-disclosure and in-depth self-expression is now taking place. Often, lots of memory work is done as members share stories about the lives of the people who have died by suicide. Interactions between members become more intense and emotional.

At this point, you as leader may have to become more supportively confrontive with any potential problem members who try to detour the group from its primary purposes. Also during this phase, group members may begin to work more actively on helping themselves and others learn new ways of coping with the absence of those who died.

Leadership roles during this phase include:

- continuing to model listening, openness, and caring.
- being supportive of continued participation of group members.
- assisting the group in dealing with any conflicts and problems that might evolve.
- making appropriate adjustments to content and meeting structure for improvement of the group.
- allowing and encouraging the group to be more self-responsible.

PHASE FOUR:
Commitment to continued healing and growth

During this phase, many members begin to ask for and reach out to others for mutual help and support. The group ambiance often becomes more relaxed and convivial. Members feel safe and at home in the group.

While you should not withdraw as leader, you should be able to share more and more responsibility with group members. You will notice group members modeling empathetic caring responses and trying to crystallize for the group new insights into the grief journey.

Remember—not every group meeting will go smoothly. You will have some good meetings, some great meetings, some not-so-good meetings, and maybe even some bad meetings. Try not to judge yourself when not-so-good or bad meetings occur.

Phase Four is clearly the most valuable phase in the life of the grief support group. In some ways, if the prior phases have been moved through, it's like the group is now on autopilot. Earlier concerns and developmental phases have been achieved, and the group is moving at a faster pace. Respect and trust levels are often way up, which then allows member to share what they need to share.

At this phase, the group process is typified by much more open-ended expression of thoughts and feelings. Activities you have planned may need to be eliminated as the group seems to need more time for open discussion. By this time members are genuinely concerned about the wellbeing of other members. Any missing members become a focus of discussion. Participants will want to know, "Why isn't Mary here tonight?"

Members also openly share their own encounters with grief during this phase. Participants take a more active role in their own healing and talk of how the group has helped them see themselves in an honest way. Group members will also often express their feelings of closeness to other members during this phase. In sum, the group's members have encountered their individual, personal grief—thanks in large part to the interdependence of the group experience.

Primary leadership roles during this phase include:

- continuing to model listening, openness, and caring.
- being supportive of continued participation of group members.
- modeling of shared leadership principles.
- assisting the group in dealing with any conflicts and problems that might arise.
- making appropriate adjustments to content and meeting structure as the group evolves.

PHASE FIVE:
Preparation for and leaving the group

Obviously, the suicide grief support group that progresses through the above four phases of development fosters mutual support and assists members in ways frequently lacking in our mourning-avoidant culture. Also obvious is that the kind of intimacy developed in the support group environment can create natural problems of separation when the group must come to an end.

Careful attention must be paid to the importance of this ending. After all, the group's closure is another loss for the group members. Many grief support groups are so successful they resist ending. However, graduation from a grief support group is an important step toward reconciliation of the suicide death of someone loved.

Expect a certain amount of ambiguity of feelings about the ending of the group. Ending may elicit withdrawal in some, sadness in others, and happiness in yet others. A theme of general optimism and feelings of progress and healing should override any natural feelings of loss. As group leader, you will need to be sensitive to any and all feelings connected to members leaving the group.

Reflecting on and affirming the growth that has been experienced in the group is a vital part of this phase. One or possibly two meetings should be focused on saying goodbye to each other as a group and supporting hopes for continued healing of the wounds of grief. There will probably be both some tears and some laughter as the group moves toward graduation. Enjoy this and be proud that you have effectively and compassionately led this group.

Primary leadership roles during this last phase include:

- creating safe opportunities for members to say goodbye to each other and to the group.
- recognizing and understanding the dynamics that occur when a group begins to end.
- encouraging reflection on individual and group growth related to the grief journey.
- providing referral for additional resources to those in need.
- conducting an evaluation of the group.

A reminder: this five-phase, theoretical model will be influenced by the unique personalities of your group members as well as by your own leadership style. Some groups will naturally move more quickly through these phases than others. The most important thing you can do as group leader is to ask yourself how you can make it safe for these phases to evolve. If your group is not moving forward or seems to be stuck, try to discern why the members don't feel a sense of trust or safety.

The *Understanding Your Suicide Grief* Model

We've all heard that the three keys in real estate are location, location, and location. Well, whether your group will be held in person or online, the three keys to successful grief support groups are planning, planning, and planning.

The effective group leader is a prepared and well-trained group leader. I suggest you plan each meeting much in the same way teachers prepare lesson plans: with a flexible structure and a purposeful sequencing of activities. In other words, don't try to wing it.

Throughout the years, I have found that closed-ended support groups that combine elements of education with open-ended discussion fostering mutual support work best. *Understanding Your Suicide Grief* support groups are shaped by these format components:

- closed-ended—meaning that the same group of people will meet for a specific, finite number of weeks
- education-based—meaning that learning about principles of the grief journey is part of the process
- open discussion—meaning that the educational segment of each meeting is followed by a dedicated time for open discussion that results in mutual support

In these groups, a trained facilitator provides some essential foundational education about about grief from *Understanding Your Suicide Grief* as well as allows time for open discussion and sharing. Members come together for a fixed number of sessions. As noted on page 7, this model is based on twelve sessions, but you are welcome to adapt the number of sessions to meet your group's unique needs. Everyone starts and stops at the same time, often meeting once a week for twelve weeks. People are not joining or leaving the group midstream. This type of group gives members a strong foundation of basic grief and mourning principles that will help them embark on a healthy path through the wilderness and maintain momentum long after the group has ended. What's more, members have the chance to meet, bond, and graduate together. This creates a strong, cohesive group dynamic.

After this closed group has ended, it's common for now-bonded members to continue to meet regularly for more informal support and possibly join up with past graduates of the same initial support group experience. This type of open-ended, less structured, ongoing group can be a wonderful source of long-term, ongoing support.

Following is a model set of twelve meeting plans that interface with *Understanding Your Suicide Grief* and *The Understanding Your Suicide Grief Journal*. These meeting plans are only intended as suggested guidelines. There's lots of room for your ideas and

RITUAL OF RECEPTION

Over the years I've discovered the value of a simple spiritual practice I use to prepare my heart and soul to be present to grievers with humility, unknowing, and unconditional love. I have come to refer to this practice as my "readiness to receive" ritual.

Just before I see anyone for support in their journey—including before group meetings—I center myself in a quiet place, inside or outside the Center for Loss and Life Transition.

Once I have gone quiet, I repeat a three-phrase mantra to myself:

"No rewards for speed."
"Not attached to outcome."
"Divine momentum."

These words help me slow down, recognize my role is to help create momentum for the griever to authentically mourn, and remember the vital importance of being present to people where they are instead of where I might think they need to be. After repeating these phrases for two to three minutes— almost in meditation—I find it helpful to reflect on the eleven tenets that undergird my philosophy of companioning the mourner (see page 3).

I encourage you to try my ritual of reception or create your own. Anything that helps prepare you to be present to grievers and embody the companioning philosophy will work.

embellishments. Be creative and consider coming up with some of your own activities that you think would serve the needs of your unique group.

My experience suggests that the format that follows encourages members to actively participate in the hard work of mourning and provides them a comforting structure that promotes open exploration. (Of course, my hope is that it also helps you as leader!)

Please note that the during the first meeting, you should be prepared to pass out copies of *Understanding Your Suicide Grief* and the companion journal to all participants. If you order all the books as a set from the Center for Loss, you will receive a discounted price, which you can then pass along to group members. Call (970) 226-6050 or visit www.centerforloss.com to order.

Between each session, group members will have homework. They'll be asked to read a section from *Understanding Your Suicide Grief* and complete the corresponding journal chapter. This support group model works best if participants do indeed take the time and energy to fill out their journals as completely as possible. Not only does journaling provide them with a healthy way to mourn, but it also creates a record of their evolving grief and their support group experience.

But not everyone is a journaler. I can foresee that at least one or two of your group members will be reluctant to fill out the journal— perhaps even refusing to complete this part of the homework each week. You know what they say—you can lead a horse to the guided questions, but you can't make them write down the answers. So if one or more of your group members won't journal, that's OK. Just encourage them to read the text and at least read through and consider the journal questions between meetings. Alternatively, you could ask them to speak their responses into a voice recorder or type them into a computer file instead of handwriting them in the book. And try not to allow the non-journaler's laxity to influence the rest of the group; if others see that the journaling is optional, they may be inclined to let it slip as well. Keep reminding your group members of the value of the journaling process.

SUPPORT GROUP MEETING PLAN
SESSION ONE
Introduction to the Group

Introduction/Welcome

Welcome the participants to the meeting and provide a brief orientation to the purpose of the support group. The introduction and orientation could include comments such as the following (if you are using a co-leader, as I hope you are, you will of course say "we" instead of "I"):

- Thanks so much for coming to this group. I welcome each and every one of you. As you know, this group will be a combined education-support group. We will be using the second editions of the books *Understanding Your Suicide Grief* and *The Understanding Your Suicide Grief Journal.* As the group leader, I believe you will find that these resources will be supportive and bring you hope.
- Each of our meetings will last ninety minutes; we will meet every week for twelve weeks. The first half of the meeting will be a discussion based on some content from the books. The second half of each meeting will be left open for group sharing.
- At tonight's meeting, we will begin to get to know each other, distribute the books, and go over our group groundrules. Before we get started, does anyone have any questions or concerns? Again, thank each and every one of you for being here tonight.

Next, you will distribute a printed list of the group groundrules you have created prior to the first meeting (See sample list of groundrules, p. 27). The group will then review the groundrules and ask questions or share concerns. Your group may wish to make changes or additions to this list.

Following a review and discussion of the groundrules, you as facilitator can model introducing yourself. If you are a suicide loss survivor, you can share a little about your experience and why you are leading this support group. Then you can invite others to do the same. Essentially, you are asking them to say who they are, who in their life has died by suicide, and a little about why they want to be in the group. Obviously, part of your role is to bring sensitivity and encouragement to the group members.

Acknowledge that participants can say as little or as much as they like. However, it is helpful to give some suggested time frame for each person to talk: "Each of us will take three to five minutes or so." Trust in the process, and don't panic when some members take more time than others. Some members may talk more initially out of anxiety, while others will appear withdrawn and may even have to pass.

Again, trust in the process. If a member feels the need to pause for a while, the group will understand. Tears need not be forced but certainly will be accepted if they occur (and they often will). If necessary, you may gently remind the group not to interrupt with questions or interpretations when members are first introducing themselves. At this first meeting, the sharing process is an important initial step in creating a supportive, healing group experience. As people tell their stories, a powerful bonding often begins. Go slowly. As I always say, "There are no rewards for speed." Listen, learn, and begin to create divine momentum toward healing.

At the conclusion of the group sharing, you will distribute copies of the two books (the second editions of *Understanding Your Suicide Grief* and *The Understanding Your Suicide Grief Journal*) to each person. Explain to members that the first book is for reading and the journal is for expressing their thoughts and feelings about what they read. Explain that the books introduce the concept of the ten touchstones—or "wisdom teachings"—that are essential physical, cognitive, emotional, social, and spiritual actions for you to take if your goal is to heal in grief and find continued meaning in living.

HOMEWORK:

Everyone is asked to read the Introduction to both resources as well as Touchstone One in *Understanding Your Suicide Grief* before the next meeting. Invite and encourage the members to complete the journal for these sections (through p. 24). Obviously, group members should be asked to come prepared to discuss the material and their reactions to what they have both read and written. I also suggest that members should be asked not to read ahead in the books; reading the primary book and completing the journal step by step will be a shared group experience. Finally, each person should be asked to bring to the next meeting a photograph of the person who died. You can invite them to attach the photo to page 6 of the journal if they wish to (size may or may not allow this). They will be asked to share the photos at the next meeting.

Again, thank everyone for being a vital part of this group, and let them know you look forward to seeing them next week.

SESSION ONE NOTES

SUPPORT GROUP MEETING PLAN
SESSION TWO

Introduction and Touchstone One

I suggest that you start this meeting by having members share the photos they brought. As directed on pages 5-6 of the journal, you might ask each of them to tell the name of the person who died, their relationship to the person, and what this particular photo captures about the unique life and personality of the person who died. Obviously, this group sharing of photos helps members get to know the people who died at the same time it helps the grieving person begin the long but necessary process of fully acknowledging the death. Be aware that one or more participants may choose not to share a picture (for various reasons). When this happens, still gently offer them the opportunity to share about the person who died.

Following the photo sharing, you will lead a discussion of the reaction to the Introduction and Touchstone One. The bulk of the discussion will probably come from the facilitative journal questions outlined in the corresponding journal sections.

You will almost certainly find that there are too many questions in the journal sections each week to go through them one by one during the meeting. Instead, I suggest you pick out three or four of the questions in advance that best seem to address the needs of this unique group and lead a discussion about them. There will be time in the second half of the meeting for group members to talk about whatever they want to talk about, which might include some of the journal questions not covered in the first half of the meeting. Use remaining questions at your discretion to encourage open exploration, discussion, and group sharing.

KEY TOPICS (FROM THE JOURNAL) FOR DISCUSSION:

• *Dosing your pain*

Suicide grief is typically profoundly painful and overwhelming. What have group members learned about the need to "dose" their pain?

• *Setting your intention to heal*

You might consider asking each group member in turn to read what he or she has written in response to the journal question on pages 20-21. This can be a powerful motivational discussion that sets the tone for the healing to come.

• *Shock versus denial*

Invite group members to share their experiences with feelings of shock and denial. What types of denial have some of the members experienced or witnessed in others they know? How are they gently and in doses working to soften any long-term denial?

• *Grief is not a disease*

Discuss the ways in which group members have taken (and are taking) steps to help themselves begin to heal.

Use your group support qualities and skills to facilitate the discussion each and every week. Approximately the second half of this and every following session should be used for open-ended discussion. However, do remember that each group meeting will have its own unique tone and dynamic. Allow each session to flow naturally.

HOMEWORK

For the next meeting, each participant should be asked to read Touchstone Two—Dispel Misconceptions About Grief (pp. 41-61) and complete the companion journal section (pp. 25-48).

SESSION TWO NOTES

SUPPORT GROUP MEETING PLAN
SESSION 3

Touchstone Two—Dispel Misconceptions about Grief

After initial warm-up, I suggest that you lead an open discussion of the grief misconceptions outlined in Touchstone Two. There is enough content here that discussion usually comes easily to members. They often like to give examples of how they have experienced these misconceptions in their own journeys.

Again, use the questions outlined in the journal to encourage open exploration, discussion, and group sharing. This journal chapter has many, many questions—too many to cover during group. Pick just a few and concentrate on those, then if there's time, continue the discussion using more of the questions.

KEY TOPICS (FROM THE JOURNAL) FOR DISCUSSION:

• *The difference between grief and mourning*

On a chalkboard or flipchart, make two columns. Title one "Grief" and the other "Mourning." The purpose here is to make sure that group members understand the difference between the two, and to help them focus on not only grieving the death, but mourning the death. Get examples of grief and mourning and write them in the appropriate column. (For example, sadness would go under grief; crying would go under mourning.)

• *All suicide loss survivors feel guilty*

Facilitate a discussion about suicide and guilt. Be certain that you are not prescribing to group members that they SHOULD feel guilty. The purpose of this discussion is to explore any potential feelings of guilt that might exist as well as the tendency for others to assume that suicide loss survivors feel guilty. Discuss the difference between blame and responsibility.

• *Explore the various misconceptions*

Go right down through the list of the different misconceptions and see what comes up in discussion. Several of the misconceptions will usually spark quite a bit of discussion and further bond your group.

A reminder that the second half of the session should be used for open-ended discussion.

HOMEWORK

For the next meeting, each participant should be asked to read Touchstone Three—Embrace the Uniqueness of Your Grief (pp. 63-84) and complete the companion journal section (pp. 49-82).

SESSION THREE NOTES

SUPPORT GROUP MEETING PLAN
SESSION FOUR

Touchstone Three—Embrace the Uniqueness of Your Grief

After initial warm-up, I suggest that you lead a discussion of the unique influences on grief outlined in Touchstone Three. On a whiteboard or flipchart, write the eleven "whys" listed in this touchstone. (You might also include a twelfth heading called "other"; this creates a place for you to write down group responses that don't fit in any of the eleven "whys.") Just by looking at the whiteboard, the group can then easily recall the twelve influences and explore the various questions related to them in their journals.

Time will probably not allow participants to explore each question under every "why," so use your judgment in processing them. Depending on your group size, you may want to break into two groups. Your skills in group process are part of the art of leading this group and making decisions about how to best run each meeting.

KEY TOPICS (FROM THE JOURNAL) FOR DISCUSSION:

• *The circumstance of the suicide (Why #1)*
This can be a difficult topic for participants. But it's helpful to talk about it and get support from fellow group members. Obviously, you will model active listening and support the unfolding process. People may feel it helpful to simply read some of what they have written about this in their journals.

• *Your relationship with the person who died by suicide (Why #2)*

Referring to the prompts in the journal (pp. 54-57), ask participants to share their thoughts or stories about their unique relationships with the person who died.

Obviously, you can facilitate discussion around the additional "Whys" and invite members to brainstorm other "Whys" as well. A reminder that the second half of the session should be used for open-ended discussion.

HOMEWORK:

For the next meeting, each participant should be asked to read Touchstone Four—Explore Your Feelings of Loss (pp. 85-131) and complete the companion journal section (pp. 83-102).

SESSION FOUR NOTES

SUPPORT GROUP MEETING PLAN
SESSION FIVE

Touchstone Four—Explore Your Feelings of Loss

This meeting is about all the various feelings participants might have as part of the grief experience. As you know, these feelings can be all over the map. Some people feel angry, some feel numb, some feel ashamed. Most people feel a combination of feelings, and these feelings change from day to day and week to week. Keep in mind as you lead this meeting that feelings are not good or bad, they just are. Model supportive, non-judgmental responses for the rest of the group.

After the warm-up, list the feelings described in Touchstone Four on the chalkboard or flipchart:

• Shock, Psychic Numbing, Dissociation, Denial, Disbelief

• Disorganization, Confusion, Searching, Yearning

• Anxiety, Panic, Fear

• Explosive Emotions

• Guilt, Regret, Self-Blame, Shame, Embarrassment

• Sadness, Depression, Loneliness, Vulnerability

• Relief, Release

Now lead a general discussion in which group members share the feelings they've had as part of their grief experience. You could then mark one area of the room for each of these feelings, then ask members to go stand in the section that represents their strongest feeling on this particular day and have the people in each cluster discuss their experience with that feeling.

Another way to broach this discussion would be to give each group member a small sticky-note tablet and have them write down the feelings they've had, one per page. Then have them stick the sticky notes up and down their sleeves. You're having your group "wear their hearts on their sleeves!" That's a good thing, because it's a metaphor for healthy mourning (expressing your grief outside yourself)!

This can lead to a discussion that not only affirms the normalcy and naturalness of each of these feelings but also encourages group members to express these feelings in some way—to not only grieve, but to mourn.

A reminder that the second half of the session should be used for open-ended discussion.

IMPORTANT:
Touchstone Four covers clinical depression. Even though you may not be a trained or licensed therapist, as group leader it is your responsibility to help identify group members who may be in need of additional help. If this or any group discussion reveals signs of clinical depression or suicidal thoughts, wait until the end of the group meeting and ask to talk individually to the group member. Share your concerns and offer to help link them with extra help. Then follow up outside of class.

HOMEWORK:
For the next meeting, each participant should be asked to read Touchstone Five—Understand the Six Needs of Mourning (pp. 133-149) and complete the companion journal section (pp. 103-124).

SESSION FIVE NOTES

SUPPORT GROUP MEETING PLAN
SESSION SIX

Touchstone Five—Understand the Six Needs of Mourning

Try starting this meeting by writing the six central needs of mourning on a whiteboard or flipchart. Each member can refer to the list as they talk about these central needs with the group.

THE SIX NEEDS OF MOURNING

1. Acknowledge the reality of the death.

2. Embrace the pain of the loss.

3. Remember the person who died.

4. Develop a new self-identity.

5. Search for meaning.

6. Let others help you—now and always.

The journal questions for Touchstone Five may help participants teach each other about how they are working on these needs. Again, invite but don't force anyone to talk. The other participants will listen and learn.

Some questions you might ask could be:

- Does one of these needs feel most prominent in your grief right now?

- Are you struggling with one of these needs more than the others?

- How is your self-identity changing as a result of the death?

- How are you accepting support from others?

- What "why" questions do you have about the death? (Field responses and write the on the board.)

- How are you at accepting support from others?

If, after the group has had the opportunity to talk about the six central needs of mourning, one or more of the six needs has not been discussed, you may bring it up. Pay particular attention to the sixth need: let others help you—now and always. Discussion about this need can once again emphasize that healing in grief is a forever process, not an event, and one that requires help from others. Even after this group concludes, members will need continued support in doing the work of mourning.

It's also a good idea for you as group leader to reiterate and emphasize the concept of "dosing" yourself with the six needs of mourning. They are not needs that you can work on one at a time and complete, checking them off your list. You will always need to revisit the six needs, and, like grief itself, none will ever be totally finished.

A reminder that the second half of the session should be used for open-ended discussion.

HOMEWORK:

For the next meeting, each participant should be asked to read Touchstone Six—Recognize You Are Not Crazy (pp. 151-178) and complete the companion journal section (pp. 125-134). If they have a linking object (you'll probably need to explain what this is; see p. 168 in *Understanding Your Suicide Grief*), ask them to bring it to the next meeting for sharing and discussion.

SESSION SIX NOTES

SUPPORT GROUP MEETING PLAN
SESSION SEVEN

Touchstone Six— Recognize You Are Not Crazy

Am I going crazy? This is such a common question for mourners to ask. Some of your group members may even have posed this question in group by now. Of course, the answer is almost always no. Normal grief just feels like insanity sometimes.

Start off this meeting by having everyone show and talk about the linking objects they brought from home. People may have brought articles of clothing, trinkets, photos, sporting goods— just about anything can be a linking object! Have members talk about why they are important to them. Affirm how natural and healing it is to have linking objects near.

After the "show and tell," ask the group members to place their objects on a table at the front of the room. For the remainder of this meeting, those objects will be a visual reminder of the special people who died as well as a way to honor the losses.

Next comes a presentation of the "going crazy" experiences listed in Touchstone Six. You may want to write the following items on the whiteboard or flipchart:

- Sudden Changes in Mood
- Memory Lapses and Time Distortion
- Polyphasic Behavior and Thinking Challenges
- Psychic Numbing, Dissociation, Disconnection
- Self-Focus or Feeling Selfish
- Rethinking and Restorative Retelling of the Story

- Powerlessness and Helplessness
- Loss of Energy and the Lethargy of Grief
- A Feeling of Before the Suicide and After the Suicide
- Expressing Feelings More Openly Than in the Past
- Griefbursts
- Crying and Sobbing
- Linking Objects and Memorabilia
- Suicidal Thoughts
- Drugs or Alcohol Use
- Dreams or Nightmares
- Mystical Experiences
- Anniversaries, Holidays, and Special Occasions
- Ritual-Stimulated Reactions, Seasonal Reactions, Music-Stimulated Reactions, and Age-Correspondence Reactions

This touchstone, like many of the others, could spur a discussion that could last for hours. You must use your discretion about where to take the discussion. Your group members may also teach you where the discussion should lead. Above all, be flexible and attentive to their needs.

You may find that the topics of dreams and mystical experiences are good ones to end with. While dreams about the person who died can sometimes be disturbing, they are often pleasant and reassuring. Mystical experiences also tend to be positive. Closing with this discussion may help group members leave this meeting feeling uplifted and hopeful.

A reminder that the second half of the session should be used for open-ended discussion.

IMPORTANT:

Touchstone Six covers the topic of suicidal thoughts. It is appropriate for you to devote a few minutes of this meeting to a discussion of suicidal thoughts. You might ask: Has anyone here had suicidal thoughts since the death? Tell us about them. Helping group members distinguish between normal, passive thoughts of one's own death and active suicidal plans may also be appropriate. Even though you may not be a trained or licensed therapist, as group leader it is your responsibility to help identify group members who may be in need of additional help.

If this discussion reveals signs of active suicidal thoughts, wait until the end of the group meeting and ask to talk individually to the affected group member. Share your concerns and offer to help link them with extra help. Then follow up outside of class.

HOMEWORK

For the next meeting, each participant should be asked to read Touchstone Seven—Nurture Yourself (pp. 179-200) and complete the companion journal (pp. 135-150). Also ask each group member to jot down one self-care tip—one they actually use themselves and that works for them—and bring it to the next meeting. They'll be asked to share their tip with the group during Session Eight.

SESSION SEVEN NOTES

SUPPORT GROUP MEETING PLAN
SESSION EIGHT
Touchstone Seven—Nurture Yourself

Try opening this meeting with a presentation of the self-care tips brought by the group members. One by one, go around the room and have each person present their self-care tip and how it has helped them during their grief journeys.

As group facilitator, one of your tasks is to emphasize how important good self-care is during a time of grief. Good self-care, in all of the five realms mentioned in this chapter, lays the foundation for any healing to come. For example, if you're not taking care of yourself physically, it's easy to see how your physical complaints (fatigue from lack of sleep, illness, pain, etc.) could distract you from—or seem to supersede—your grief. Or if you're not meeting your social needs, you're probably not getting the necessary outside support. This touchstone is an important one because without it, all the others will fail.

Next, write Nurturing Your Whole Self across the top of the whiteboard, then make five columns or five separate pages on flipchart paper:

Physical

Cognitive

Emotional

Social

Spiritual

Divide your group members into five smaller groups and assign each group one of the five aspects of self. Ask each group to come up with a list of doable, practical ways that mourners could nurture themselves in their assigned area. The litmus test for an idea to make it on the list is the question: Would I actually try this? If the answer is yes, group members should put the idea on the list. If the answer is...well, probably not...tell them not to put it on the list. The lists should also include any ideas that group members themselves have actually used and benefited from.

After each small group has had twenty minutes or so to generate their lists, have them present them to the group at large. Add ideas that other group participants vocalize during this presentation. (You might consider collecting all the tips generated tonight, typing them up, and emailing them to the group or distributing them as a handout during the next meeting.)

Additional discussion points can come from the journal questions for Touchstone Seven.

Some questions you might ask could be:

- How is your body responding to your grief?
- Did anyone draw a grief map (journal p. 144) that they'd like to share with the group?
- What gives you pleasure and joy in your life?
- Have your friendships or your social circle changed since the death?
- How do you nurture your spirit?

A reminder that the second half of the session should be used for open-ended discussion.

HOMEWORK
For the next meeting, each participant should be asked to read

Touchstone Eight—Reach Out for Help (pp. 201-220) and complete the companion journal section (pp. 151-164).

SESSION EIGHT NOTES

SUPPORT GROUP MEETING PLAN
SESSION NINE

Touchstone Eight—Reach Out for Help

One definition of mourning is that it is the "shared social response" to grief. In other words, it is not only grief expressed privately outside oneself—by crying, journaling, making art—it is also grief expressed publicly outside oneself—by talking to others, hugging and holding someone else, participating in a support group, etc.

Congratulate group members on being part of a grief support group. By coming to group meetings and sharing their thoughts and feelings with others, they are helping themselves activate Touchstone Eight—Reach Out for Help.

Ask: "Whom do you turn to for help? And how are you proactively reaching out versus expecting others to approach you with support?" This discussion, in addition to the journaling they have already done on this topic, can help group members see that there are a number of people in their lives they can rely on for love and support. Sometimes group members just need a little encouragement accessing that support—opening up to the people who love them and being more forthcoming and proactive about their needs.

The "Rule of Thirds" (*Understanding Your Suicide Grief*, p. 205) is another good topic of conversation for this group meeting. The rule of thirds says that about one-third of the people in your life turn out to be neutral when it comes to your grief, one-third are toxic to the healing journey, and the final third are empathetic grief helpers. This is a good time and place for your group members to vent about the toxic third. Encourage them to tell stories about how others have made them feel ashamed of their grief, judged them in negative ways, said hurtful things, etc. (You can also refer to their responses to the journal question about the crazy things people say and do, journal p. 134.)

Note that this chapter also contains information on determining if mourners might want to look into individual counseling as well as signs and categories of complicated grief. It's appropriate for you to bring up these topics during group discussion; it gives members who are having a particularly difficult time an opportunity to consider whether they might need the additional support of a grief counselor.

Try reviewing the risk factors sometimes associated with complicated grief (unique circumstances surrounding the suicide, a close or dysfunctional relationship with the person who died, difficulty expressing grief, excessive substance use) as well as the categories of complicated grief (unembarked grief, impasse grief, off-trail grief, encamped grief) and asking participants to talk about any points of connection they feel. (See *Understanding Your Suicide Grief*, pp. 217-219.)

If any group members see themselves as needing or being interested in individual grief counseling, or if they identify their grief as complicated, offer to talk with them after the session about next steps. Help them recognize that getting extra support is not a sign of weakness. Indeed, it is a sign of great strength.

Finally, this chapter discusses the role of suicide grief support groups. Here you are leading a (I hope) thriving, healing group. By now the group dynamic should be strong and loyal. If you feel confident that your group is working well, a good closing activity for this meeting might be to ask group members how they feel about the group and how it is helping them. If you think you might get more candid responses from an anonymous opportunity to talk about the group, pass out blank sheets of paper and ask each group member to write down one or two or three things about how they have found the group to be helpful. Give them five minutes to write, then collect the papers and with their permission you as leader can read them aloud.

A reminder that the second half of the session should be used for open-ended discussion.

HOMEWORK:

For the next meeting, participants should be asked to read Touchstone Nine—Seek Reconciliation, Not Resolution (pp. 221-232) and complete the companion journal section (pp. 165-172).

SESSION NINE NOTES

SUPPORT GROUP MEETING PLAN
SESSION TEN

Touchstone Nine—Seek Reconciliation, Not Resolution

This is the meeting in which you focus on the concept of reconciliation in grief. I say that people don't "get over" or "recover from" their grief; instead they learn to "reconcile" themselves to it. In other words, they learn to accommodate the loss as part of who they are and proceed in their lives with meaning, purpose, and happiness.

You might begin with an open-ended discussion of where people see themselves in the healing process. Then, walk down through the listed signs of reconciliation (p. 225) and see what discussion follows.

Key topics for discussion:

- Ask members what reflections they have about the concept of "reconciliation" versus "resoluton" in grief.

- Facilitate a conversation surrounding the concept of "not attached to outcome." How do group members relate to this concept?

- Create an open-ended discussion about hope, faith, and trust in God/Higher Power.

This chapter also explores the role of hope in healing. The main text tells you that living with hope is living in anticipation of a good that is yet to be. The journal asks journalers if they have hope for their healing. How is hope playing a role in the experience of group members at this time? Lead a discussion about hope and its presence (or absence) in the hearts of group members today.

A reminder that the second half of the session should be used for open-ended discussion.

HOMEWORK:

For the next meeting, participants should be asked to read Touchstone Ten—Appreciate Your Transformation (pp. 233-242) and complete the companion journal section (pp. 173-180).

SESSION TEN NOTES

SUPPORT GROUP MEETING PLAN
SESSION ELEVEN

Touchstone Ten—Appreciate Your Transformation

The journey through grief is transformational. When you leave the wilderness of your grief, you are simply not the same person you were before you entered it.

How are you changing as a result of this suicide, and in what ways are some of these changes positive growth? This is the topic of session eleven.

While the concept of transformation and growth can be challenging, the reality of change is more neutral. Some questions you might ask the group at this meeting include:

- How is your day-to-day life changing?

- How are your spiritual beliefs changing?

- How are your relationships with others changing?

- How are your values changing?

- What new attitudes, insights, and skills have you discovered?

Don't forget to remind group members that while suicide grief does often result in growth, it is not growth we masochistically go looking for. The death is not "justified" by the growth group members may describe. (You may want to spend a few minutes talking as a group about how everyone feels about the price they had to pay for this growth.)

You might write down the different "Growth Means..." for everyone to see on the board or a flipchart. Invite people to express which of these they can most relate to and believe are becoming part of their life experience.

This chapter also reviews the concept of purpose in life. Ask your group if they believe they have a purpose in life and if so, to please share it with the group. This will often lead to interesting and heartfelt discussions about goals for the future—which is an important topic for your group to review at this point. (After all, you only have one meeting left!) Given this opportunity, group members will often encourage one another in their intentions to do something about their newfound (or newly strengthened) purposes.

Another discussion-worthy topic explored in this chapter is our responsibility to live after we come to grief. I say that mourners have a responsibility to live and live purposefully, not only for themselves but also on behalf of the person who died. This is also a challenging statement, and not everyone believes as I do.

Do your group members agree? If so, how does this responsibility affect their grief and their lives? If not, why not? Before they leave, you might ask group members to write a list of one thing they could do in the coming week on behalf of the person who died. Ask them to report on that thing at the next and final meeting.

A reminder that the second half of the session should be used for open-ended discussion. Keep in mind you should be helping members prepare to graduate from the group. This is your next-to-last meeting, and you will want to be conscious of the preparation for leave-taking in the group. Go back and reread about the support group's developmental phases, looking specifically at Phase Five and your leadership role (pp. 50-52 in this book).

HOMEWORK

Group members have already completed reading *Understanding Your Suicide Grief* and filling out the companion journal. So there is no homework per se for the coming week. You might consider if there is any activity you would like them to do in the coming week. For example, you could ask participants to write a generic letter to a future class of grief support group members. The next time you run a group, you could read these letters of encouragement and support as icebreakers at your first session. It might also be a good idea for you to ask group members to bring snacks or treats to share at the next meeting, since it is kind of a goodbye gathering.

Do ask members to reflect on what the group experience has been like for them. You will commonly see some expressions of resistance to the reality that the group will end next week. Use your helping skills to help the group openly acknowledge any thoughts and feelings related to this potential reluctance.

SESSION ELEVEN NOTES

SUPPORT GROUP MEETING PLAN
SESSION TWELVE
Graduation

Graduation—it's always a bittersweet occasion. It's a time of ending as well as a time of new beginnings. For your suicide grief support group members, it's a time to say thank you and goodbye, and reemerge into their lives.

It's appropriate to remind your group that though the support group is ending, their grief is not. As you've no doubt discussed many times by now, grief never discretely ends. And their need to mourn the death openly and honestly and continue to receive support from others certainly does not end after this final session. Be conscious of helping members identify additional sources of support in your community. Other members may need to talk out their plans to graduate to an open-ended support group or individual counseling.

This meeting is also about graduation. Encourage each member to express what they feel was gained from this group experience. You may consider having each participant give a verbal gift to a fellow participant. This is a positive comment a member has observed about a fellow member during the support group. Each person is encouraged, but not forced, to participate in this verbal gift-giving.

As part of the graduation, you may also want to give certificates of support group completion to each member. See p. 93 of this book for a sample certificate. Feel free to creatively amend it to suit your needs. For a PDF printable version, please contact us at (970) 226-6050 or centerforloss.com. Share food and drink, and openly discuss whatever is on your group members' minds and hearts.

Group members who want to stay in touch with each other can be encouraged to share their phone numbers or e-mail addresses with one another. Or you can take charge of this role by asking those who are interested to write their names, phone numbers, and e-mail addresses on a piece of paper you'll pass around. After the meeting you can type up the list and email it to everyone who signed up.

Thank everyone for attending the support group and reinforce that you hope each member has been helped in their healing journey. If you think appropriate, provide each graduate with a copy of *365 Days of Understanding Your Grief*. While not specific to suicide loss, these daily readings tied to the ten touchstones will provide ongoing support and comfort in the days ahead.

Provide copies of the Support Group Evaluation Form (see pp. 110-111), and ask everyone to complete one before they leave. Their feedback will be invaluable in helping you plan for future groups.

Conclude this meeting with refreshments and time for mingling and socializing.

Pat yourself on the back. You have just completed a successful suicide grief support group!

SESSION TWELVE NOTES

CERTIFICATE OF *Support Group* PARTICIPATION

Be it known that on this day,

has completed the *Understanding Your Suicide Grief Support Group* and has immersed themself in the Ten Essential Touchstones for finding hope and healing their heart.

You have given and received support from fellow group members.

Your presence and sharing of your experience with loss have touched the lives of many, and for that we are grateful.

We wish you continued healing and hope for renewed meaning and joy in your life.

Group Facilitator

Date

TOUCHSTONE ONE
Open to the Presence of Your Loss

TOUCHSTONE TWO
Dispel Misconceptions about Grief

TOUCHSTONE THREE
Embrace the Uniqueness of Your Grief

TOUCHSTONE FOUR
Explore Your Feelings of Loss

TOUCHSTONE FIVE
Understand the Six Needs of Mourning

TOUCHSTONE SIX
Recognize You Are Not Crazy

TOUCHSTONE SEVEN
Nurture Yourself

TOUCHTONE EIGHT
Reach Out for Help

TOUCHSTONE NINE
Seek Reconciliation, Not Resolution

TOUCHSTONE TEN
Appreciate Your Transformation

Responding to Problems
in the Group

Murphy's Law ensures that no suicide grief support group will run smoothly one-hundred percent of the time. Problems will arise, typically due to one of three reasons:

1. **LACK OF LEADER PREPARATION**
    "Where are we supposed to meet?" "How long was this meeting supposed to last?" "I thought *you* were going to bring the name tags!" If administrative details aren't properly taken care of, group members will feel left in the lurch. On the other hand, problems can also arise when a leader is too controlling. In general, a lack of effective leadership skills can result in a number of negative consequences. Proper grief support group facilitator training will help you prepare to lead and avoid these problems.

2. **DISCREPANCIES BETWEEN GROUP MEMBERS' EXPECTATIONS AND LEADER'S EXPECTATIONS**
    Each individual group member will have their own expectations for the group. The place to vocalize these various expectations is in your prescreening process and during the group review of the groundrules in the first session. If mutual expectations aren't clarified early on, the group is set up for failure.

3. **INDIVIDUAL PARTICIPANT PROBLEMS**
    Each person brings a unique personality and history to the group. No matter how well you prescreen members, you will encounter challenging participants who will test your skills as group leader. Effective intervention in these cases requires that you first establish a caring, trusting relationship between you and each group member.

    Following are descriptions of some of the more common challenging participants you're likely to encounter in your groups. I've suggested ways you might deal with each of them, but do keep in mind that confronting an individual member in front of the rest of the group is rarely a good idea. Instead, ask to meet with them individually after the meeting.

Sometimes group members will themselves intervene by confronting another member about problems arising in the group. When this happens, it's appropriate for you to take charge of the conversation. Use your paraphrasing and perception checking skills to clarify what is being said (and perhaps to state it more supportively), then move on. Speak to the participant individually after the meeting.

And remember, even when you must confront, lead with your heart and with compassion. Usually, difficult participants are just teaching you about their personalities, their unique ways of interacting with others, and complications of their loss and grief journeys.

AMY THE ABSENT

Amy is the group member who is there but not there. Sometimes this person is still in the initial shock wave from the death and is simply unable to speak. Amy may have tried to attend the support group too early in her grief journey, or she may just need the group to be patient and understanding as she acclimates and her sense of shock/ numbness softens. However, there are also Amys who consciously choose not to participate and interact with the group in passive-aggressive ways: "I'm here, but I don't plan to be a part of this group."

APPROPRIATE WAYS TO INTERVENE: From the very first session on, make an effort to help everyone feel involved and part of the group. Create safe ways to invite the Amys in, such as asking, "Amy, I'm wondering what your week has been like since we met last?" Making eye contact even when this person is quiet is also a way of engaging her and inviting her participation. If your Amy is outright passive-aggressive, you may need to talk to her individually and explore whether the group can appropriately meet her needs at this time. You may discover that some people are just very shy, quiet, or overwhelmed—yet they perceive they are getting a lot out of the group experience. Sometimes if you can help them let the group know this, the group can embrace and accept them for the quiet people they are.

ANN THE ADVICE-GIVER

Even if you have a group groundrule that says, "Do not give advice unless it is asked for," you will probably have an Ann in one of your groups at some point. Ann is quick to inform others what they should do to solve problems. She may try to take over under the guise of being helpful.

APPROPRIATE WAYS TO INTERVENE: Take a few minutes to remind the group at large about the difference between supportive listening and advice-giving. Give examples. When necessary, you can also gently remind Ann of the groundrule about advice-giving. Or you can even ask, "Did you feel that John needed you to tell him what to do about his concerns?" Obviously, the goal is to prevent advice-giving in your group unless it is asked for. We know that many grieving people resent unsolicited advice.

ALBERT THE ACADEMIC

Albert is the intellectual in the group and often likes to show off his huge knowledge base. He might quote a recent article he read or expose a little-known theory to explain his, or more likely someone else's, behavior. Analysis and interpretation are Albert's joys in life! There may be a condescending quality to his tone; generally he thinks he knows more than most anyone else in the group.

APPROPRIATE WAYS TO INTERVENE: Initially, I often allow Albert's natural defense mechanism to help him ease into the group. However, when it becomes a consistent pattern, it can be destructive to the group. Therefore, I sometimes try saying things like, "Albert, you have really helped us understand what the articles say, but sometimes I wonder how you feel." Of course, he may lack insight, but it's worth a try. Sometimes when I know my relationship with Albert is strong, I'll say to him privately, "Albert, I know that I sometimes have a tendency to intellectualize things that are emotionally and spiritually painful for me. I wonder if you see that same tendency in yourself?"

BOB THE BLAMER

Bob is the participant who projects that other group members (or other people in general) are the ones who cause his problems. Often this self-defeating thought pattern has been in his coping-mechanisms toolkit for some time. Bobs often projects an accompanying sense that no one has ever understood him, and no one ever will. This self-crippling stance wears thin very quickly with members who are trying to honestly look at themselves and sort out new directions in their lives.

APPROPRIATE WAYS TO INTERVENE: Compassionately attempt to help Bob become more self-responsible and eliminate the tendency to blame. Try a private, tentative comment like, "Bob, sometimes I'm struck by how you find fault with others. I'm wondering what would happen for you if you looked inside yourself at times instead of outside?" A supportive confrontation like this has the potential of getting Bob more connected to himself and can help him start to make positive changes.

CHARLENE THE CHALLENGING

Charlene is the participant who likes to challenge the leader. She might accuse you of not knowing what you are doing, which in turn may cause you to question yourself. Charlene likes to put you on the spot and tries to make you look incompetent in the eyes of group. Her challenges are more often made in front of the group instead of privately.

APPROPRIATE WAYS TO INTERVENE: Be certain you don't get defensive when the challenges come forth. This is just what Charlene wants and would probably lead to more challenges. It's often appropriate to acknowledge her comment but then offer to talk with her after group so you can better understand one another. While you may be tempted to initiate a dialogue in front of the group that will prove your competence, resist the urge. The group will most often respect your decision to deflect the criticism in the moment and discuss the situation individually with Charlene.

FRED THE FORCED

Fred is the group member who is there because someone else wants him there. He has no intention of participating and feels he is being forced by a spouse or friend. He hopes everyone will forget he is present and will leave him alone. Fred rarely makes eye contact with anyone, particularly the group leader. If questioned or invited to participate, he often passes and looks put upon. If Fred is attending with a spouse or friend, he often defers questions to them.

APPROPRIATE WAYS TO INTERVENE: Try to screen this person out in your prescreening process because their presence will be counterproductive if not outright damaging to the group. Once Fred is in the group, however, you can attempt to make him feel welcome and warmly invite his participation. If that doesn't work, the group will be well-served if you meet with Fred individually and explore the possibility of him leaving the group. You may also consider referring Fred to individual counseling, but he will usually resist this suggestion.

HOLLY THE HOLY ROLLER

Holly spends so much time talking about heaven that people wonder if her feet are on the ground! While faith values and spirituality are very important and should absolutely be explored in a suicide grief support group, the Hollys of the group often alienate other members with their my-way-or-the-highway dogma. Holly usually projects a lack of any personal problems and may perceive other members' pain as a "lack of faith." She may also judge or frown upon others' spiritual beliefs.

APPROPRIATE WAYS TO INTERVENE: Support that what works for one person may not work for another. You can accept how important Holly's faith is to her while also (with appropriate timing and pacing) helping her and the group acknowledge that spirituality is highly individual and that having faith and mourning are not mutually exclusive. If Holly is advice-giving about the need for everyone to have faith like hers, you must gently remind her of the groundrules and redirect the group in ways supportive to everyone present.

IVAN THE INTERRUPTER

Ivan is the group member who, consciously or unconsciously, is always interrupting other people. He can't seem to keep his mouth shut. Other participants will begin to see it coming and may start hesitating to share for fear they will be interrupted. Ivan must be helped to control his interrupting tendencies or he will destroy the very heart of the group.

APPROPRIATE WAYS TO INTERVENE: Gently remind Ivan of the equal time groundrule. When this fails, meet with him individually and say something like: "Ivan, I notice that sometimes you have a tendency to interrupt the person who is talking. Are you aware of this?" You can then offer to give him a signal when he interrupts; this can often be done in good humor with excellent results.

PAUL THE PREACHER

Paul has a lot in common with Holly, but he often preaches about anything and everything—not just religion. The group experience provides Paul with an audience. He may attempt to dominate the group as he tells the group what they should and should not do. He is usually very well-intentioned but tends to wear thin with the group. He may seem overly rehearsed, as if he has preached his message many times.

APPROPRIATE WAYS TO INTERVENE: Gently remind Paul of the equal time groundrule as well as the advice-giving groundrule. You might express how his tendency to preach impacts you. Say, for example, "Sometimes when I listen to you, Paul, I wonder if you really want to hear what others think and feel." Again, this supportive confrontation must be done privately and is intended to help him reflect on how he is impacting the group.

RALPH THE RAMBLER

Ralph is a close cousin of Paul the Preacher — he just changes subjects more often. Ralph tends to bore the group as he rambles on yet seems to say little of substance related to the needs of the group. He rarely completes his sentences in ways that allow others to talk; he just keeps running on and on and on. The group kind of lets out a silent groan as soon as Ralph utters his first words. Without a doubt, one rambling Ralph can ruin your group if you don't effectively intervene.

APPROPRIATE WAYS TO INTERVENE: Once again, return to the groundrules related to equal time. If this fails, step up your efforts to help Ralph by being supportively direct about his tendency to talk a lot. The group will often be able to help if you ask them if anyone was able to follow what Ralph just said. There is some risk in this approach in that a fellow group member may attack Ralph for rambling on all the time and saying little. Again, if all else fails, ask to speak with Ralph after the meeting and attempt to compassionately help him look at his rambling and become a more concise, discerning contributor to the group.

SARAH THE SOCIALIZER

Sarah's goal is to keep the group from getting too serious about anything. The problem here, of course, is that grief will bring about serious, thoughtful, painful discussions. Sarah may see the group as an opportunity to be with other people and socialize in a fun way. Obviously, her expectations are different than the group's. Sarah may laugh or change the subject when everyone else is sad, or she may make inappropriate comments to distract the group from the work at hand.

APPROPRIATE WAYS TO INTERVENE: First, understand that many people protect themselves from getting hurt by trying to stay in a social mode or using levity to avoid intimacy. Try well-timed, sensitive comments like, "I notice that sometimes you laugh when others are sad. How do you understand that about yourself?" Or, "When I see you laugh like that, I wonder what you are feeling?" Some Sarahs will lack insight into their use of socializing, while others will appreciate your efforts to help them.

WALLY THE WE-SAYER

Wally attempts to talk for everyone in the group or to be the group spokesperson. "We think we should . . ." is a common lead for this person. Wally assumes (and this is what creates problems) that everyone thinks and feels the same as he does. Allowing the "we" messages to continue often causes quieter members to give in to the "we talk" Wally espouses. Resentment can grow, and some members will probably drop out and not even tell you why.

APPROPRIATE WAYS TO INTERVENE: Ask Wally if he is speaking for every person in the group, or try asking the group if there is anyone who doesn't agree with Wally's statement. If it is healthy, your group will provide a safe atmosphere for people to express their unique thoughts and personalities. Gently confronting Wally often helps achieve that goal.

Again, even when you must confront challenging participants , lead with your heart and with compassion. Usually, participants are doing the best they know how to do and reflecting their unique personalities.

RED FLAGS SUGGESTING REFERRAL FOR INDIVIDUAL COUNSELING

There are some grieving people whose current grief needs will be met more effectively in individual counseling or therapy. The following "red flags" should alert you to the need for making an appropriate referral.

- Persistent thoughts of suicide, expressions of serious suicide intent, or the development of a specific suicide plan
- Arriving at your group under the influence of alcohol or drugs
- Previous diagnosis of a serious mental health disorder
- Profound symptoms of anxiety or depression that interfere with the ability to do basic self-care
- Uncontrollable rage directed at others
- Physical harm to self or others
- Uncontrollable phobias, such as an inability to be by themselves at any time
- Entrenched symptoms of mourning (such as anger or guilt) that do not appear to soften at all over a period of months

The above list is not exhaustive, of course. You should use your good judgment as to whether or not a group member would benefit more from individual counseling than from a support group at this time. It is also important for you as a group leader to realize that, even when you make a referral for individual counseling, the person may choose not to take your advice.

Evaluating
Your Group's Progress

"Progress" in grief is difficult to pinpoint. Grief is something we never truly "get over"; it is an ongoing, recursive process that unfolds over many weeks and years. So, if your twelve-week support group is finishing up and you feel unable to quantify each member's progress, don't feel discouraged.

First, listen to what your heart tells you about the progress the group has made. Have you felt a growing sense of trust among members? Have members been able to share their experiences in ways they wouldn't have been able to elsewhere? Have you noticed particular members are able to open up more or cope better than they were when the group began? Have members thanked you for starting the group or shared with you how much it has helped them?

Next, ask group members for feedback in the form of an end-of-group evaluation form like the one at the end of this book. People often feel more comfortable expressing in writing what they can't bring themselves to say face-to-face.

Finally, consider the grief needs every mourner has and how the group has helped members work through those needs. Instead of the "stages of grief"—a term that makes grieving sound like a simple one, two, three process—I use the model that follows. You covered the six needs of mourning with the group in session six, but here I'm exploring how you can also use the six needs as a group facilitator tool, to help you discern how the group has helped members move toward integrating the loss into their lives.

The Mourner's Reconciliation Needs of Mourning

NEED 1. ACKNOWLEDGE THE REALITY OF THE DEATH

This need involves encouraging the group memebers to gently confront the reality that someone loved has died and will not return. Some members will have begun to meet this need before they enter the group. In fact, members acknowledge the reality of the death just by attending group meetings. What I find, though, is that the support group experience helps them acknowledge the reality more deeply, moving from head to heart. Did you see this happening in your group? How so?

NEED 2. EMBRACE THE PAIN OF THE LOSS

This need involves encouraging the group memebers to embrace all the thoughts and feelings that result from the suicide death of someone. We all need permission to mourn. Sometimes what we need most from others is an awareness that it is OK to talk out our many thoughts and feelings, no matter what they are. Support groups provide a safe place in which to explore thoughts and feelings—even the most difficult ones. Did you see this happening in your group? How so?

NEED 3. REMEMBER THE PERSON WHO DIED

This need involves allowing and encouraging the group members to pursue a relationship of memory with the person who died. Memories that are precious, dreams reflecting the significance of the relationship, and living legacies are examples of some of the things that give testimony to a different form of a continued relationship. Support groups can help meet this need by encouraging:

- the sharing of memories, both spontaneous and through specifically designed group activities.

- the presentation of linking objects and photos.

- journal writing between group sessions.

My experience in learning from thousands of suicide loss survivors is that remembering makes hoping possible. The survivor's future becomes open to new experiences and relationships to the extent that past memories have been embraced. Did you see this happening in your group? How so?

NEED 4. DEVELOP A NEW SELF-IDENTITY

Part of your self-identity comes from the relationships you have created with other people. When someone you care about dies, then, your self-identity is naturally affected. Your grief group members may have gone from being wives or husbands to widows or widowers, for example, or from being parents to bereaved parents. More broadly, this need is about group participants figuring out who they are now.

Support groups help meet this need by allowing members to talk out their thoughts on self-identity challenges and changes and explore them with others in similar situations. Did you see this happening in your group? How so?

NEED 5. SEARCH FOR MEANING

Your support group members may naturally ask many "Why?" questions about the suicide death that have affected them. Why did this happen? Why now? Why in this way? Support groups help by providing a safe, nonjudgmental place in which to search for meaning.

With support and understanding, grieving people usually learn that human beings cannot have complete control over themselves and their world. They begin to befriend impermanence and become more comfortable with vulnerability. They often learn that faith and hope are central to finding meaning in whatever one does in this short life. And they develop a renewed appreciation for life and what it has to offer. Did you see this happening in your group? How so?

NEED 6. LET OTHERS HELP YOU—NOW AND ALWAYS

As noted, grief is an ongoing process that unfolds over the course of many weeks and years. So, while your support group may have lasted only for a finite number of weeks, your group members will still need continuing support from others.

For some members, this may mean taking part in the same group next year or the year after. (You can help them decide if that is appropriate.) For others, it may mean continuing informal relationships with other group members; lifelong friendships often spring from grief support groups. Still others will leave your group ready to rely on other people and systems for support. In any case, it's a good idea to for you to compile a list of community resources that people leaving your group can turn to for additional support in the months ahead.

During the course of the group, did you see participants open more and more to the support of one another? Did you see an awareness blossom of the benefits of reaching out for and accepting help from others? How so?

Suicide Grief Support Group Member Evaluation Form

What impact has this group experience had on your grief journey?

What were the most valuable aspects of this group experience for you?

What did you learn about "where you are" in your grief journey right now?

What changes have you seen or experienced in yourself that you might be able to attribute at least partially to this group experience?

What are some of your perceptions of the group leaders and their style of leadership?

Is there anything about this group and how it was conducted that you wish could have been different?

How did your participation in this group impact your significant relationships at home and with friends?

If you could describe in a sentence or two what this group meant to you, what would you say?

Suicide Grief Support Group Leader Self-Evaluation Form

How did you feel in leading this group?

What were some of your initial impressions of this group? Did these impressions change over time? If so, how?

Which, if any, members did you have more difficulty with than others? Do you have any sense of why this was?

Which leadership skills did you use and work on, and what was the outcome?

What did you learn from this group?

What was it like working with this co-leader in this group?

Is there anything about this group experience that you wish could have been different?

What changes will you make for any future groups you lead?

What additional areas of leadership training might you benefit from?

Caring
for the Caregiver

Like you, I'm proud of the work I do with grieving people. At the same time, I've discovered that good self-care is essential for me to truly be present to those I wish to help. This is the caregiver's conundrum: How do we care well for others while at the same time caring well for ourselves? Perhaps, like me, you are aware that you may be good at meeting the needs of everyone else but tend to ignore or minimize your own need for self-care. If so, this chapter should be of help to you!

So Why is Excellent Self-Care Essential?

For caregivers to suicide loss survivors, good self-care is critical for at least three major reasons.

First and most important, we owe it to ourselves and our families to lead joyful, whole lives. While caring for grieving people is certainly rewarding, we cannot and should not expect our work to fulfill us completely.

Second, our work is draining—physically, cognitively, emotionally, socially, and spiritually. Assisting bereaved people is a demanding interpersonal process that requires much energy and focus. Whenever we attempt to respond to the needs of those in grief, chances are slim that we can (or should) avoid the stress of emotional involvement. Each day we open ourselves to caring about mourners and their personal life journeys. And genuinely caring about people and their families during times of great loss touches the depths of our hearts and souls. We need respite from such naturally draining work.

And third, we owe it to those we help. My personal experience and observations suggest that good self-care is an essential foundation of caring for and meaningfully companioning people in grief. They are sensitive to our ability to "be with" them. Poor self-care results in distraction from the helping relationship, and grieving people often intuit when we are not truly present to them.

Poor self-care can also cause caregivers to distance themselves from people's pain by trying to act like an expert. Because many of us have been trained to remain professionally distant, we may stay aloof from the very people we are supposed to help. Generally, this is a projection of our own need to stay distant from the pain of others, as well as from our own life hurts. The expert mode is antithetical to compassionate care and can cause an irreparable rift between you and the grievers in your care.

So, does this work have to be exhausting? Naturally draining, yes, but exhausting? I don't think so. Good helpers naturally focus outward, resulting in a drain on both head and heart. You will hear some people say, "If you do this kind of caregiving, you might as well resign yourself to eventually burning out." Again, I don't think so. The key is to practice daily, ongoing, nurturing self-care.

A number of suicide grief support group leaders have told me that a framework that they have found helpful to explore related to their self-care needs can be found in my book, *Companioning You! A Soulful Guide to Caring for Yourself While You Care for the Dying and the Bereaved.* You will be able to reflect on three important areas of loss awareness:

1. Your Background Related to Death and Life Losses
2. Your Current Personal Issues Surrounding Grief and Loss
3. Your Motivations as a Caregiver

Self-Care Guidelines

The following self-care guidelines are not intended to be cure-alls, nor will they be appropriate for everyone. Pick and choose those tips that you believe will be of help to you in your efforts to stay physically, cognitively, emotionally, socially, and spiritually healthy.

Remember, our attitudes about stress and self-care sometimes make it difficult to make changes. However, one important point to remember is that with support and encouragement from others, most of us can learn to make positive changes in our attitudes and behaviors.

You might find it helpful to have a discussion among other caregivers about caregiver fatigue syndrome. Identify your own signs and symptoms of burnout. Discuss individual and group approaches to self-care that will help you enjoy both work and play.

The Joy of Mini-Vacations

What creative ideas can you come up with to renew yourself? Caregivers are notorious for helping others create self-care time while neglecting their own needs. Here are a few ideas to get you started. However, I encourage you to create your own list and take action.

- Schedule a massage with a professional massage therapist.

- Have a spiritual growth weekend. Retreat into nature. Plan some alone time.

- Go for a drive with no particular destination in mind. Explore the countryside, slow down, and observe what you see.

- Treat yourself to a night in a hotel or bed and breakfast.

- Visit a museum or a zoo.

- Go for a hot-air balloon ride.

- Take an afternoon off and go to the movies—maybe even a kid's movie.

- Go to a yard sale or auction.

- Shoot hoops in the driveway.

- Go rollerskating or rollerblading with a friend.

- Enjoy a photographic retreat. Take your phone or camera into nature and shoot away.

- Watch cartoons with a child.
- Visit a farmer's market and shop for fresh produce.
- Drop by a health-food store and walk the aisles.
- Go dancing.
- Take a horseback ride.
- Plan a river-rafting trip.

What self-care ideas can you come up with?

REMEMBER YOUR CHILD-LIKE SELF

Have you ever met an overly serious grief caregiver who projects gloom and doom? Odds are they have forgotten the vitality and enthusiasm of their childhood years. Let's pause and recall some of the characteristics of childhood.

CHILDREN:
- are physically connected to the world around them.
- take risks.
- are open, enthusiastic learners.
- imagine and dream.
- are naturally curious.
- spontaneously laugh and smile a lot.
- are passionate and expressive.
- try new things when they get bored.
- rest when they need rest.
- try to have fun whenever they can.

So, have you "grown up" and forgotten about the joys of being a child? If so, you may have left behind some of the best self-care strategies ever. Think about the way healthy kids go about their day, then think about how you spend your day. Have you forgotten how vital fun is to life and living?

There is a well-established link between play and energy. Playing often can be a vital part of your self-care plan. Being grown-up doesn't mean always being serious. Most really successful people not only work hard, they also play hard. Childlike behavior generates joy, fun, and enthusiasm. Ask yourself: What can I do to stay in touch with my inner child?—then jot down a few ideas here:

_____

_____

_____

_____

Work Smart, Not Hard

Many caregivers never had the opportunity to learn essential time-management skills that result in working smart, not hard. You may find the following helpful:

Create specific goals for personal and professional development. Parse your annual goals into monthly goals. Break up your weekly goals into daily goals. Ask yourself, "What do I want to accomplish this year, this month, this week, this day?" Planning each day can give you a roadmap to getting to your destination!

Do one thing at a time. Caregivers are notorious for trying to do and be all things to all people and all projects all the time. Quality always suffers when you multitask or take on too much.

End the day by planning for tomorrow's projects whenever possible. That way, you'll not only waste less time getting started the following morning, you'll also arrive at work feeling more in control of the day ahead.

Protect yourself from constant interruptions. When you're working on a task, nothing will sabotage you more than interruptions. Block out the necessary time to complete tasks.

Work when you work best. We all have certain natural peak hours of performance. Pay attention to your inner clock. Are you a morning person or a night person? Does a brief nap recharge you?

Focus and reject. This is a reminder to stay focused on the task at hand. Learn to switch off those things that prevent you from accomplishing desired tasks. Sometimes this means delaying or returning calls, emails, and texts. If you always stay available, you won't have time to accomplish what you may really want and need to.

When all else fails, retreat to a hideout. When working on project development, you may need to find a safe, quiet place where you can hole up with no interruptions. Tell only those who truly need to know where you are. You'll be amazed at what you get done.

When you know your energy level is dropping, take a break. After a ten-minute walk or a short nap, you may be able to accomplish much more than you could have otherwise.

Delegate tasks whenever possible. Watch out for busywork that might be done more efficiently with the help of technology tools or by someone else.

Throughout the day, ask yourself, "What's the best use of my time right now?" Focus on those tasks that need to be done first. This requires discipline but will pay many dividends.

Build Support Systems

Working with grieving people requires a natural outward focus: on the needs of those we attempt to help. When we're feeling drained, it's important to have sounding boards and support. Ideally, supportive colleagues and friends provide:

Unconditional acceptance and empathy. In other words, friendship, understanding, and nurturing.

Help with complicated situations. Assistance with problem-solving and troubleshooting when we encounter challenging people and circumstances in our support groups.

Mentoring. Encouragement to continue to receive education and develop new tools to assist us in our work. Models that inspire us and remind us of the importance and value of our work.

Challenge. Encouragement to stretch ourselves beyond our current limits.

Referrals. Good caregivers will recognize occasions when it's appropriate to refer support group members for individual counseling and other forms of assistance. They'll also be connected to area caregivers and can make referrals.

Ask yourself, can I seek support systems when I need to? Who are

the people in my life that make up my support system? List five
people you could turn to right now for support and nurturing.

Are you involved in any relationships that are damaging to you?
What would happen if you placed some boundaries on these
relationships?

Review your current support system and make an honest assessment of how well it meets your needs. Identify areas where you could use some changes.

Remember the Importance of Spiritual Time

I have found that nurturing my spirit is critical to my work as a bereavement caregiver. Spiritual time helps me combat fatigue, frustration, and life's disappointments. To be present to those I work with and to learn from those I companion, I must appreciate the beauty of life and living.

Spiritual, quiet moments or downtime (for me, often spent in nature) recharges my spiritual energy. While you may embrace your spirit differently than I do, I encourage you to ask yourself: How do I renew my spirit?

Some people do this through prayer and meditation. Others go hiking, biking, running, fishing, or taking part in other forms of physical solitude. Obviously, there is no one right way to renew your spirit. But to companion grieving people, we must each find ways to relight our divine sparks.

I've always found profound meaning in the words of Carl Sandburg:

> A man must get away
>> now and then
>> to experience loneliness.
>
> Only those who learn how
>> to live in loneliness
>> can come to know themselves
>> and life.
>
> I go out there and walk
>> and look at the trees and sky.
> I listen to the sounds of loneliness.
> I sit on a rock or stump
>> and say to myself
>> "Who are you Sandburg?
>> Where have you been,
>> and where are you going?"

So, I ask you to ask yourself: How do I keep my spirit alive? How do I attend to my divine spark? How do I appreciate the good, the beautiful, and the truthful in life?

Listen to Your Inner Voice

As a caregiver to mourners, you may at times experience grief overload (too much death, grief, and loss in your day-to-day life). The natural demands of this kind of work can cause you to have tunnel vision about death and grief. For example, if your own child has a headache, you may immediately think *brain tumor*. If your partner complains of heartburn, you think *heart attack*.

I'll never forget the time I returned home from a three-day lecture series on childhood grief to find my office manager had scheduled the following day full of counseling a variety of grieving people and two dying children and their families. Sitting there looking at the schedule, my inner voice called out, "I can't do any more sadness right now. I need and deserve a spirit break." So, I rescheduled all the appointments and spent the day driving through nearby Rocky Mountain National Park. I returned home in the late afternoon and spent the remainder of the day playing with my children and being present to my wife.

Caregiving presents you with the gift of an enhanced awareness of the many tragedies that touch people's lives. Just as those you companion are changed by death, you are changed by their experiences as well. To remain connected to our deep appreciation for life and love, we must stay grounded—and that means caring for ourselves as we care for others.

Beautiful color wallet cards of the Caregiver's Self-Care Manifest are available to order at www.centerforloss.com.

A Self-Care Manifesto for Bereavement Caregivers

We who care for grieving people have a wondrous opportunity: to help others embrace and grow through grief—and to lead fuller, more deeply lived lives ourselves because of this important ministry.

But our work is draining—physically, cognitively, emotionally, socially, and spiritually. We must first care for ourselves if we want to care well for others. This manifesto is intended to empower you to practice good self-care.

1. **I deserve to lead a joyful, whole life.**
   No matter how much I love and value my work, my life is multifaceted. My family, my friends, my other interests, and my spirituality also deserve my time and attention. I deserve my time and attention.

2. **My work does not define me.**
   I am a unique, worthy person outside my work life. While relationships can help me feel good about myself, they are not what is inside me. Sometimes I need to stop doing and instead focus on simply being.

3. **I am not the only one who can help grieving people.**
   When I feel indispensable, I tend to ignore my own needs. There are many talented caregivers in my community who can also help the bereaved.

4. **I must develop healthy eating, sleeping, and exercise habits.**
   I am aware of the importance of these things for those I help, but I may neglect them myself. A well-balanced diet, adequate sleep, and regular exercise allow me to be the best I can be.

5. **If I've been overinvolved in my caregiving for too long, I may have forgotten how to take care of myself.**
   I may need to rediscover ways of caring for and nurturing myself. I may need to relearn how to explore my own feelings instead of focusing on everybody else's.

6. **I must maintain boundaries in my helping relationships.**
   As a caregiver, I cannot avoid getting emotionally involved with grieving people. Nor would I want to. Active empathy allows me to be a good companion to them. However, I must remember I am responsible to others, not for others.

7. **I am not perfect, and I must not expect myself to be.**
   I often wish my helping efforts were always successful. But even when I offer compassionate, on-target help, the recipient of that help isn't always prepared to use it. And when I do make mistakes, I should see them as an integral part of learning and growth, not as measurements of my self-worth.

8. **I must practice effective time-management skills.**
   I must set practical goals for how I spend my time. I must also remember Pareto's principle: twenty percent of what I do nets eighty percent of my results.

9. **I must also practice setting limits and alleviating stresses I can do something about.**
   I must work to achieve a clear sense of expectations and set realistic deadlines. I should enjoy what I do accomplish in helping others but shouldn't berate myself for what is beyond me.

10. **I must listen to my inner voice.**
    As a caregiver to the bereaved, I will at times become grief overloaded. When my inner voice begins to whisper its fatigue, I must listen carefully and allow myself some grief downtime.

11. **I should express the personal me in both my work and play.**
    I shouldn't be afraid to demonstrate my unique talents and abilities. I must also make time each day to remind myself of what is important to me. If I only had three months to live, what would I do?

12. **I am a spiritual being.**
    I must spend alone time focusing on self-understanding and self-love. To be present to those I work with and to learn from those I companion, I must appreciate the beauty of life and living. I must renew my spirit.

A Final Word

With appropriate preparation and a compassionate heart, you can and will help many grieving people find hope for their healing in your suicide grief support groups. They will feel safe to express their grief, which will provide them with divine momentum toward integrating the loss into their lives. They will be transformed—"an entire change in form."

Facilitating grief groups not only transforms members, it transforms leaders. Remember to honor your own transformation. You have likely grown in your own wisdom, your own understanding, and in your own compassion.

I wish you well, my friends and colleagues.

Selected Reading List

Chen, M., Rybak, C.J. *Group Leadership Skills: Interpersonal Process in Group Counseling and Therapy, 2nd edition.* SAGE Publications, Inc., 2017.

Coenen, C. *The Creative Toolkit for Working with Grief and Bereavement: A Practitioner's Guide with Activities and Worksheets.* Jessica Kingsley Publishers, 2020.

Friends for Survival, Inc. *Pathways to Purpose & Hope: A Guide for Creating a Sustainable Grief Support Organization for Families and Friends After a Suicide Death.* Friends for Survival, Inc., 2020.

Graves, D. *Setting Up and Facilitating Bereavement Support Groups: A Practical Guide.* Jessica Kingsley Publishers, 2012.

Hansen, S. *Grief and Loss Support Group Facilitator's Manual.* CreateSpace Independent Publishing Platform, 2015.

Hedtke, L. *Bereavement Support Groups: Breathing Life into Stories of the Dead.* The Taos Institute Publications, 2012.

Hoy, W.G. *Bereavement Groups and the Role of Social Support: Integrating Theory, Research, and Practice.* Routledge, 2016.

Wolfelt, A.D. *Companioning the Bereaved: A Soulful Guide for Caregivers.* Companion Press, 2006.

Wolfelt, A.D. *Counseling Skills for Companioning the Mourner: The Fundamentals of Effective Grief Counseling.* Companion Press, 2016.

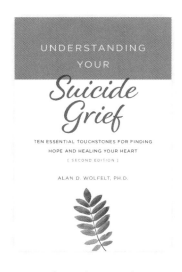

Understanding Your Suicide Grief

Since its debut in 2009, this favorite by one of the world's most respected grief counselors has found a place in the homes and hearts of thousands of mourners across the globe.

Filled with compassion and hope, *Understanding Your Suicide Grief* helps you understand and befriend your complex, yet normal thoughts and feelings after the death of someone loved. *Understanding Your Suicide Grief* is built on Dr. Wolfelt's Ten Touchstones—basic principles to learn and actions to take to help yourself engage with your grief and create momentum toward healing. This second edition includes concise include concise additional wisdom on new topics such as the language of suicide grief, a framework to understand complicated grief, grief overload, the significance of activating events, soulmate grief, the loneliness of grief, and more.

If you're grieving a suicide loss, this refreshed resource will be your compassionate companion as you journey through the wilderness of your unique grief.

ISBN: 978-1-61722-335-8 • 270 pages • softcover • $14.95

ALL DR. WOLFELT'S PUBLICATIONS CAN BE ORDERED BY MAIL FROM:
Companion Press | 3735 Broken Bow Road | Fort Collins, CO 80526
(970) 226-6050 | www.centerforloss.com

The Understanding Your Suicide Grief Journal

This companion workbook to the second edition of Dr. Wolfelt's resource *Understanding Your Suicide Grief* helps you explore the many facets of your suicide grief through guided journaling. After you read a section in *Understanding Your Suicide Grief*, the journal asks you questions about what you've just read. It invites you to consider, clarify, and jot down your thoughts and feelings.

A good grief journal is a safe place of solace—somewhere you can express yourself no matter what you are experiencing. If you're grieving a death by suicide, this journal and its companion text will help you understand and embrace your grief, actively mourn, and move toward healing. You'll find that the journal can also be used to help honor the person who died and/or work through any lingering relationship issues.

As you express your emotions in this journal, you will feel them beginning to soften as well as become more integrated into your ongoing life.

ISBN: 978-1-61722-337-2 • 200 pages • softcover • $14.95

ALL DR. WOLFELT'S PUBLICATIONS CAN BE ORDERED BY MAIL FROM:
Companion Press | 3735 Broken Bow Road | Fort Collins, CO 80526
(970) 226-6050 | www.centerforloss.com

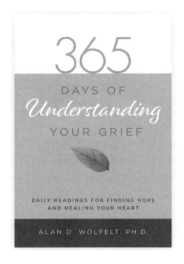

365 Days of Understanding Your Grief

After a significant loss, grief is an everyday experience. But through conscious reflection each day, you can remind yourself that grief, while painful, is a normal, necessary part of your love for the person who died.

Those who grieve will find comfort and understanding in this daily companion. These one-page-a-day readings will help you feel supported and encouraged to mourn well so you can go on to live well and love well. Written as a companion to his classic title *Understanding Your Grief*, this gem can be read in concert or as a standalone book. As you engage with the regular doses of guidance, you will discover reflections that invite you to relight your divine spark.

Reading just one page each day will help you sustain hope and heal your broken heart. For the next year, allow this little book to be your steadfast support and companion.

ISBN: 978-1-61722-299-3 • 384 pages • softcover • $14.95

ALL DR. WOLFELT'S PUBLICATIONS CAN BE ORDERED BY MAIL FROM:
Companion Press | 3735 Broken Bow Road | Fort Collins, CO 80526
(970) 226-6050 | www.centerforloss.com